O change me, touch me with youth, alchemize me!
Let fiery melody blaze and twirl in my breast;
Life-fire leap into esctasy! Let night's ribs crack;
Let skies, as they fill with dawning enlightenment,
Raise terror in remotest dark.

From today I shall fight to seize and carry aloft your conch of victory.

—Rabindranath Tagore

Bhagavad Gita

The Eternal Song Goes On

A TRANSLATION FOR THE NEW MILLENNIUM

by

VIJAYA ACHARYA

First published by Sacred Arts Trust 1997,
courtesy of the Karnani family, London

Second edition published by Sacred Arts Trust 2021

Designed by Matthew Parkinson
Set in Cormorant Garamond

Cover image: Mandala by Tophan Maharana

The Sacred Arts Trust, registered charity 1044763,
works for the preservation of temple arts and culture.

www.sacredartstrust.org

SACRED ARTS TRUST

Table of Contents

Preface

The earth is meant to serve as a field for Divine Sacrifice. Humanity holds a central place in the entire cosmic order; if greed, anger, hatred and fear, deified and concentrated in the nuclear arsenals currently being stockpiled by Earth's various factions, are allowed to consume us, then this sacred field will be desecrated, all sacrifice will be stopped and the entire cosmic order will be imperilled.

Our knowledge of, and faith in, the transcendent must not divert us into an uncaring other-worldliness. Indeed, when this world is transformed fully, when the elements of the so-called mundane environment are seen as the paraphernalia of sacrifice, when they are completely engaged as such by a fully conscious devotee, then they become transfigured into pure spirit – the profane is seen to be sacred, the mundane alive with transcendental life.

The mythic record, as contained in the Puranas and their cousins in various traditions, reveals to us our *dharma*, the duty inherent in our times, our shared responsibility. We must be partners in the planetary and universal salvation. Theologically, we must understand that there can be no absolute evil, but there must be absolute good; in this lies our hope.

The governments of men within the historical period have neither embodied nor adequately represented the eternal and absolute good. There is much of relative good and much of relative evil in all of the competing world views and systems, and thus the current struggle between East and West, North and South, presents no clear-cut mythic archetypes, clearly identifiable from any absolute perspective, at least. Simple non-alignment with the major power blocks is no guarantee of true alignment with the will of absolute goodness. Pious hearts, worldwide, have prayed, "Thy will be done on Earth as it is in absolute realm, the realm of the Supreme Godhead". The mark of anointment lies neither on the foreheads of the leftist oligarchs, nor on the worried brows of the resurgent militarists of the 'developed' West.

Earth's true heroes and 'sheroes' must arise unattached to the failed ideologies of our primitive beginnings, ready to help humanity move forward and upward in harmonious dance with our ecosystem and universal law.

The explosion of the first nuclear bomb was a signal that it was time for humanity to grow up. This new technology allowed us to act as co-destroyers and, thus, hinted at our roles as co-creators and co-preservers. It seems quite plausible that just as governments grant the full rights and responsibilities of citizenship to persons at their 21st birthdays, so the Lord has arranged that at the dawning of the 21st century of the Christian era, we would be confronted with these rites of passage.

Humanity, after millenniums of wars or uneasy 'peace', must evolve forms of co-operative behaviour that reflect the human psyche at its healthy best to replace the dangerous pathologies which have become institutionalised in the current social life of the species. Let the Spirit guide us and others who attempt to follow the path of peacemakers; may we be shown with clarity the means of progress and enlivened with an intense longing for the upliftment of all living entities.

It is our task to prospect for peace with a greater fervour than that which has animated those who have searched for gold and precious gems. Indeed, in the event of a nuclear holocaust, the entire value of all the earth's resources will be reduced to nil. So this search for peace must take precedence over all the other tasks facing human society.

There is no doubt that as more and more sincere souls dive deeply within their hearts for answers, pathways out of the existential dilemma posed by the threat of nuclear winter will present themselves.

May the blessings of God and all of the devotees always be upon us. May pure love always reign supreme in our hearts. May the all-auspicious Supreme Peacemaker continue to enthuse our efforts.

Vijaya Acharya
California, 1985

Introduction

In India, before the dawn of the Greek civilisation, an advanced God-centred society was flourishing. Under a succession of dynasties, the people lived in peace with each other and in harmony with nature. Unfortunately, just before the advent of the Dark Age (as this historical period is known by us), the rulers of many of the small kingdoms that comprised the Indian Empire became oppressive in their behaviour towards their people and began arming for war.

In the imperial capital, Hastinapura (the site of modern New Delhi), the throne of the rightful Emperor Yudhishthira had been usurped by the political intrigues of his cousin Duryodhana. Yudhishthira had been orphaned along with his four brothers on account of the untimely death of his father, King Pandu, and had been placed under the guardianship of his blind uncle Dhritarashtra. Dhritarashtra, however, favoured his own sons headed by Duryodhana, and through political intrigues had conspired to have him placed on the throne. The Goddess of the earth was herself groaning under the strain of the military build-up of these impious rulers, and she prayed to God for relief. God, the Supreme Absolute Truth, personally responded to her plea by incarnating in His original form of love and beauty, Lord Krishna, Who became the close personal friend and adviser to the Pandavas, the orphaned sons of King Pandu.

After a long series of attempts at peacemaking, in which Lord Krishna Himself participated, it became clear that Yudhishthira could return to the throne, and peace and prosperity again bless the land, only if Duryodhana and his impious, militaristic allies could be defeated on the field of battle.

In those days, the warrior class would leave the populated places, where innocent bystanders might be injured, and organise the warfare in some appropriate open space. In this case, the vast field of Kurukshetra, ninety miles north of Hastinapura, was chosen, and the huge armies of both alliances organised themselves on the respective parts of the battlefield.

Since this site was the scene of many holy sacrifices in previous days, it naturally favoured the armies of the Pandavas, who quite literally had God on their side, inasmuch as Lord Krishna had agreed to become the chariot driver for King Yudhishthira's younger brother, the noble and heroic Arjuna. Although Krishna Himself refused to take up arms in the fight, He acted as the adviser to the Pandavas. His presence on their side guaranteed ultimate victory. Nonetheless, because it was a civil war – a fight of brother against brother – the pious and soft-hearted Arjuna began to have second thoughts about the whole matter, and it is at this juncture that the holy dialogue which is called 'Bhagavad Gita' (God's own Song) begins. In this most sublime translation by Vijaya Acharya, prepared especially to help in bringing about a new and golden age, the Eternal Song goes on!

Gurupad Arjuna

Lord Krishna delivering the Bhagavad Gita to Arjuna.

THE FIRST CHAPTER

Arjuna's Despondency

While sitting nearby the great field where his sons were about to engage in conflict with his pious nephews, Dhritarashtra, the blind and ageing Monarch, inquired of his trusted secretary:

"Sanjaya, my sons and the sons of Pandu, my departed brother, have now assembled in the sacred field known as Kurukshetra. Please tell me what they have accomplished in their preparations for battle." (1)

Sanjaya, who had been enabled to envision things even at a distance by the mercy of his spiritual master, Vyasa, then began to answer, describing the scene near the military front:

"After surveying the formations into which the Pandava armies had arranged themselves, your eldest son, King Duryodhana, approached nearby his teacher, Dronacharya, and addressed him as follows:

'O my revered teacher, just cast your vision upon the mighty military forces arranged into phalanxes under the supervision of your brilliant student, Dhrishtadyumna, the son of Drupada. (2–3)

There, alongside Bhima and Arjuna, stand many valiant warriors who are practically equal in valour with them.

Yuyudhana, Virata and Drupada are amongst those great bowmen, each of whom could defeat 10,000 archers in single-handed combat. (4)

Dhrishtaketu, Chekitana, Kashiraja, Purujit, Kuntibhoja and Shaibya, all powerful heroes, pillars of the human civilisation, stand there as well. (5)

Yudhamanyu the Mighty, Uttamauja the Brave along with Abhimanyu, the son of Subhadra, and Draupadi's valiant sons are all aligned together against us. Great indeed is their prowess with bow and chariot. (6)

But now, O most cultured of men, I shall speak to you about the great commanders who have taken charge of my armies. Please take note with care. (7)

Your own good self as well as Bhishma, Karna, Kripacharya, Ashvatthama and Bhurishrava are all undefeated champions who have never failed to be victorious in battle. (8)

Many other great heroes as well are fully ready to give up their lives for my cause. All are very well armed with the most potent weaponry and are expert in the strategic aspects of warfare. (9)

There is no way to measure the full strength of our forces and, what is more, we have the shelter and leadership of our great and noble Grandfather Bhishma. Our opponents, on the other hand, have a far limited force led by the less experienced General Bhima. (10)

Now that all of our forces have been well arranged in the various parts of the field and the strategy has been well developed, I request you and all our generals to give the fullest possible co-operation to Grandfather Bhishma. Then victory is sure!' " (11)

Sanjaya continued:

"Bhishmadeva the Elder, the grandfather revered by both the armies, then blew upon his conch shell and sent a sound like the roar of a lion through the ether. Hearing this, Duryodhana became elated, relishing the thought of victory. (12)

His armies responded by simultaneously releasing an uproarious vibration of conch shells, bugles, trumpets and all kinds of drums and horns. The sound was tumultuous! (13)

Remaining on a powerful chariot drawn by cloud-white horses, Lord Krishna, the husband of the Goddess of Fortune, along with Arjuna, the second eldest of the five Pandava brothers, blew their sacred conch shells. (14)

The Master of all sentient beings, Lord Krishna, blew His conch of the name Panchajanya, and Arjuna blew his, the great conch named Devadatta. Then General Bhima, who was famous as the performer of impossible tasks and for his wolf-like appetite, blew his conch, the Paundram. (15)

The conch shell named Ananta-Vijaya, which means 'Unlimited and complete Victory', was sounded by the rightful King Yudhishthira, and the two younger Pandava brothers, Nakula and Sahadeva, then blew their horns, named Sughosha and Manipushpaka respectively. (16)

O ruler of the world, the King of Varanasi and the great warrior Shikhandi, the heroic Dhrishta-dyumna and the noble Prince Virata, Satyaki and King Drupada of the Panchalas, along with his sons as well as many other great warriors such as Arjuna's son Abhimanyu, none of whom had ever seen defeat in the field of battle, then sounded their conch shells, one after another. (17–18)

The great symphony produced by the vibration of all the Pandava horns seemed to shatter heaven and Earth, as well as the confidence in the hearts of those allied to Dhritarashtra. (19)

Thereupon, surveying the forces that had been assembled by Dhritarashtra's sons, Arjuna stood on his chariot, upon which was flying his flag emblazoned with the figure of Hanuman, the monkey-devotee of Lord Rama, and took up his bow preparing to release his arrows. O mighty King, Arjuna then spoke these words to the Lord of all beings, Shri Krishna:

'O You Whose nature is supreme perfection, please lead our chariot forward between the two armies so that I may observe the great forces that have assembled here out of their desire to make war. Let me see with whom I must struggle in the impending strife. (20–22)

I wish to see those who have come together to fight with us, desiring to endear themselves to Duryodhana, who is beset by crooked intelligence.' " (23)

Sanjaya narrated:

"O descendant of the noble line of Bharata, upon hearing the words of Arjuna, who was famed for his victory over ignorance, the proprietor of the senses, Lord Krishna, then drew their cart, which was the finest amongst chariots, forward to the middle ground between the armies. (24)

There in the foreground, not far from Bhishma, Drona and all of the great world leaders, Shri Krishna, the omniscient Lord, said:

'O beloved son of Pritha, just observe the great assembly of the Kurus.' (25)

There Arjuna could observe his fathers and grandfathers, his revered teachers and uncles, his brothers and sons, grandsons and friends, his father-in-law and his well-wishers, who were all standing there amidst the legions of the two armies. (26)

Seeing all of his relatives brought together in such perilous circumstances, Arjuna became pervaded with a great compassion for them, and while he was thus lamenting he spoke as follows:

'O Krishna, after seeing all of these, my own dear kinsmen, assembled in such a militant spirit, the limbs of my body have begun to shake and my mouth has become parched. (27–28)

My body is trembling and my hair is standing on end. My famous bow, Gandiva, is falling out of my hands whilst my skin feels as if on fire. (29)

O Keshava, O Krishna, I do not feel that I can remain here any longer. I am suffering from the shock of all this madness, which seems unable to produce anything besides the anomaly of that which we seek. O my Lord, why are we here? (30)

No good can come from killing our own relatives, and neither can I wish to become victorious in such a fight. Even upon winning, I could not derive any happiness from the kingdom thus obtained. (31)

My dear Govinda, satisfier of the senses of all, of what value will such a kingdom be? Of what value will happiness or even life itself be when all those with whom we could enjoy such a happy life have now taken up their places on the battlefield? O killer of the demon Madhu, when the lives and wealth of my revered teachers, my fathers and my sons, my grandfathers, maternal uncles, my father-in-law and all my dear friends are about to be lost, why should I desire to kill them, even if unrivalled sovereignty of the three worlds was at stake? O shelter of all, O my beloved Krishna, I can find no pleasure in the thought of fighting merely for the control of this earth. (32–35)

We will certainly incur sin for such acts, even though they be felonious aggressors. Surely the sons of Dhritarashtra, our own dear friends and kinsfolk, do not deserve death from our hands, so how, my dear Madhava, can we hope to become happy by such killing? (36)

O shelter of all beings, having been overcome by greed, they are unable to see the great fault of killing dear friends and family members. We, on the other hand, will certainly incur sinful reaction if we participate in such a struggle, knowing fully well the great crime committed by the destruction of family and dynasty. (37–38)

With the destruction of the dynasty and of the families' eternal religious values, the family will be completely overtaken by irreligion. (39)

With the rise of irreligion, the ladies of the house will become polluted, and when the flower of womanhood has thus been tainted, illegitimate and unloved children will be conceived. (40)

The entire family will then be afflicted by the hellish condition which the uncultured children will create. In such families, the obligations to make offerings for the well-being of the ancestors will certainly be neglected and our forefathers will suffer deprivation. (41)

Those who destroy family religious values devastate in turn all co-operation within the community and all social values. (42)

I have heard from authoritative sources that those who destroy family religious traditions are always kept resident in hell. (43)

O what a mysterious turn of fate it is that we proceed to commit such a great sin, being impelled by greed for the happiness enjoyed by kings. For this we are prepared to kill our own dear ones. (44)

Instead of meeting our cousin-brothers on the field of battle, it is my conclusion that it would be preferable for me to allow myself to be killed, without taking up arms or resisting!' " (45)

Sanjaya then said:

"Being deeply disturbed in mind, Arjuna then cast down his bow and arrows and sat lamenting on his chariot." (46)

THE SECOND CHAPTER

The Philosophy
of Divine Communion

"Lord Krishna, the saviour of all surrendered souls, then began to address the depressed Arjuna, whose eyes were brimming with tears on account of his feelings of mercy and compassion. (1)

The omnipotent Lord said:

'How is it that you have become polluted with such lamentation in this dangerous hour? To depart from the path of the Aryans, the truly enlightened way, will cause you to be infamous in this world and to lose the celestial pleasures of the hereafter. (2)

Arise, O conqueror of foes! Throw off this weakness of heart which is befitting only lesser men. Do not give in to becoming a eunuch, my dear son of Kunti!' (3)

"Arjuna responded:

'It is my duty to worship the feet of such great personalities as Bhishma and Drona. How can I now be expected to return fire on them, engaged on the field of battle? (4)

I would prefer to live in the world as a beggar rather than enjoy a grand life sprinkled with the blood of my gurus.

Although they lust to gain the things of this world, their position nonetheless commands my reverence. (5)

I cannot say whether it is better for us to win this war or to lose it, and neither would I care to go on living if all these cousin-brothers of ours must die. (6)

I know that this confusion which I feel within my mind in regard to my service has come about on account of certain deep weaknesses of spirit, but I have the greatest confidence in Your advice. Now I approach You for Your shelter, praying that You will accept me as Your disciple and enlighten me with suitable instructions. (7)

I am myself unable to overcome this great feeling of sorrow and lamentation which has deadened my finer sensibilities, and I feel I should be unable to do so, even if I were to be named the Sovereign Emperor of the earth, with unrivalled authority, like the celestial overlords enjoy in their domains.' " (8)

Sanjaya narrated:

"After speaking in this way, Arjuna, although famous for his enlightenment as well as for his victory in battle, then said: 'O Govinda, I cannot fight!' and became quiet. (9)

Then with a very pleasing smile upon His face, the Lord of all sentient beings, Shri Krishna, in the midst of the opposing armies gathered there, began to speak to His sorrowful friend as follows:

'Although you speak as if you were a person of great learning, you show sorrow over that which requires no such grief. Those whose vision is clear see no cause for lamentation, either for those who still share the world with them or for those who have departed from their sight. (10–11)

There was never a time when I or you were not, or when any of these monarchs assembled here were not. Neither shall a time ever arise when we shall not be. (12)

Just as we observe in this life the change of a youthful body to an old one, so yet another body is adopted at the time when this one must pass. Those who have understood the true nature of life are never bewildered by this. (13)

Joy and sorrow arise and depart just like summer and winter. None of these perceptions have any permanence, and one must therefore be perseverant in the face of all change. (14)

Many occasions for rejoicing will arise and many occasions for grief, but to you who are the best of all persons I reveal this truth that those who learn to be equal to both become eligible to obtain admission into the life everlasting. (15)

Those who have obtained a profound vision of reality by studying both what is temporary and what is eternal have reached the conclusion that that which has no permanent basis can have no real existence, whereas that which is eternal and substantial can never pass into non-existence. (16)

You should understand that there is within the body an element which pervades it and which no one shall ever be able to kill. (17)

Each living being is indestructible and beyond limitation; the eternal self shall continue, though each body must no doubt meet its end. Therefore, you should proceed to carry out your responsibilities as your great ancestor Bharata would desire you to do. (18)

Those who imagine that the self can be killed and who seek to classify the various causes of death fail to understand the truth. In fact, the living beings cannot die, and therefore nothing can kill them. (19)

The eternal spiritual personality of each individual being never takes birth and will never die. Since they are, they shall never stop being. They are beyond mundane origin and are everlasting; they are ancient yet ever-youthful, and even when these bodies become ash they survive still intact. (20)

My beloved Arjuna, for a person who has realised the imperishable quality of the eternal spiritual personalities of all living beings and who knows them to have no point of origination or termination, how can the question of killing and being killed arise? (21)

Just as one must put on new clothes when the old ones have become worn, so does each person accept new bodies when the old ones are no longer. (22)

That which constitutes the true spiritual personality of the self is beyond the power of any weapon to injure or of fire to burn. It neither becomes wettened by water, nor dried by the winds. (23)

The eternal spiritual personality, which is also known as the soul, is indivisible and undissolvable and cannot be transformed by fire or air. Each person's life is everlasting and, in their essential natures, the living souls who pervade all creation are unwaveringly steady and ever-existent. (24)

You must realise clearly that the soul, the spirit-self, lies unseen, beyond the mind's ability to conceive and beyond the range of temporal modulations. Therefore, please try to transcend your unfounded anxieties. (25)

Even if you think that the self *is* born and *does* die, there is still no necessity for you to mourn, my strong-armed friend. (26)

For, those who have been born are all certainly destined to die, and it is also a fact that all who die are born again. Therefore, it is unwise for you to mourn over the inevitable and unavoidable. (27)

Originally, no one had a manifested physical form. Although during an interim period such forms become manifest, ultimately all these beings will again be in their original state once the worlds are destroyed. On what basis then is there need for grief? (28)

There are those who are able to see and fully realise the nature of their eternal spiritual personalities, clothed in all their wonder and glory. Other faithful persons preach about the magnificence of the soul, whilst others hear such splendid descriptions with relish. However, there are also others who even after hearing about the nature of the eternal spirit-self are unable to penetrate at all into the subject matter. (29)

Since the eternal spiritual personalities who dwell within the physical forms of all creatures can never die, for what do you grieve? (30)

Your service is to protect the world's innocent people, and at this point there exists no better way to do that than to carry out your plans for battle. (31)

A member of the royal order should be joyful when an opportunity to enter so easily the gates of the heavenly paradises presents itself through circumstances beyond his control. (32)

If, therefore, you abandon duty and honour and neglect your service, failing to fight, then your fame will be tarnished and you will have to suffer sinful reactions. (33)

People all over the world will speak about your infamous character, and for a man who has once enjoyed great prestige, such a fate is worse than death. (34)

All of the great fighters assembled here will think that you have fled from the fight due to fear, and this will greatly reduce you in their estimation. (35)

It will be a cause of great distress for you to hear those who hate you slandering you and speaking of your failure and incapacity. (36)

Overcome your uncertainty and fight with your full efforts, my dear Kaunteya. If you are killed you will enter paradise, and if you prevail you will enjoy unobstructed sovereignty on Earth. (37)

Therefore, simply carry out your duty by fighting, being equal to happiness and distress, profit and loss, victory and defeat. Doing so, you will incur no blame. (38)

Thus far I have been attempting to help you to gain an intellectual comprehension of the principle of eternal spiritual personalities sojourning within matter. Now please hear from Me as I describe to you the inner attitude which must be employed if one is to transcend the bondage of fruitive works and attain mystical communion with Me. (39)

Every effort expended on the path to union with the Divine is valuable and earns progress which can never be lost. Even a very small effort made in this way will save one from the terror of repeated birth and death. (40)

Those of strong faith have only one object for contemplation, whereas the intelligence of those who lack spiritual determination is divided into many branches. (41)

Persons of limited intellect strive to follow the eloquent words of the Scriptures which point out the ways leading to the fulfilment of one's desires, the attainment of celestial regions, and the benefits and powers derived from good birth. They become involved in many elaborate ceremonies, performed only with a view to enjoying a life of opulence. (42–43)

Those whose consciousness is bewildered by the desire for material enjoyment and the glitter of worldly opulence are never able to control their minds and focus them upon the transcendence. (44)

Major sections of the Holy Scriptures deal primarily with subject matter pertinent to the interactions of the three binding forces of material nature. My dear Arjuna, you should try to exist on a plane transcendental to all such things. Eternally established in pure goodness, you must rise above the pains of this world of duality and, free from temporal desire, become fully self-realised. (45)

Just as one in need of water searches for a well yet certainly becomes satisfied encountering a great lake, so will those who seek knowledge in the scriptural texts certainly become satisfied upon encountering the Supreme Divine Person, Who is a reservoir of perfect information and the source of all the Scriptures. (46)

It is most natural that you should act, but you have no right to the fruits of your activities, and neither are you the real cause of such fruit appearing. At the same time, you must not entertain the thought of abandoning action. (47)

To attain the great calm that results from true spiritual practice, you must give up all attachment and act with a mind free from the worry which accompanies thoughts of success and failure. (48)

O winner of wealth, Arjuna, cast off at a distance all such degraded action and take shelter of a consciousness of full surrender to the Supreme Divine Person. Those who act simply desiring to enjoy the fruits are short-sighted and selfish. (49)

The true art of living lies in humanity's efforts for union with the Supreme Truth, by which endeavour souls may become free from both the rewards and punishments that arise from action. (50)

Giving up the chain of fruitive action, those who are actually wise attain the position of absolute freedom, which lies beyond the miseries of mortal existence. (51)

When your consciousness has emerged from the deep jungles of illusion, you will then consider all that you have heard in this world, or all that you may still hear, to be without real importance. (52)

You can be considered truly self-realised only when you are unwavering in your absorption in the Divine Reality and are free from the mental disturbances arising from the seeming contradictions in so many scriptural texts.' (53)

"Arjuna then inquired:

'In what way can persons whose consciousness is actually fixed in transcendental realisation be distinguished from others? What is their language like and in what way do they conduct themselves?' (54)

"The Lord replied:

'My dear child of Pritha, persons may be understood to have attained a firm hold on transcendence when they have parted with the desires for selfish enjoyment which are born of the mental flux and have become satisfied in the pure self. (55)

Never becoming aggravated by the various causes of suffering in this world, and never anxiously seeking after its pleasures, one who is free from blind attachments and the influence of anger becomes fearless and may be called a sage of sober mind. (56)

Those who are without false attachments, who never plot for special gain or despair in times of loss and trouble, may be known as truly fixed in consciousness. (57)

Just as a tortoise withdraws his protruding limbs within his shell, so should the person fixed in transcendental consciousness be able to separate the senses from their objects. (58)

There are many restrictive regulations governing the behaviour of embodied beings towards the various sense objects, but it is only when persons have been graced by a taste of higher things that they shall be able to give up all taste for the lower. (59)

My dear Kaunteya, the force of the stimulated senses is sufficient to disturb even the most discriminating of persons in the midst of all their efforts for self-control. (60)

Those whose senses have been tamed by full engagement in My loving, devotional service can certainly be known as persons who are fixed in transcendental awareness. (61)

The senses become attached to an object after beginning to dwell on it. As a result of such involvement, the desire to enjoy the object arises, and when such desire is thwarted, anger springs up. (62)

When there is anger, one becomes easily illusioned and loses memory of right and wrong. Such loss of memory then leads to the destruction of one's discriminatory abilities, which leads in turn to continued immersion in the whirlpool of birth and death. (63)

However, those who can supervise the involvement between senses and sense objects by exercising enlightened self-control, and who become free thereby from craving and from false repression, very soon attain the full blessings and mercy of the Supreme Divine Person. (64)

For those who have thus been benedicted by that sublime and sacred Mercy, misery ceases to exist. My devotees culture a happy state of mind in which their intelligence becomes more and more profoundly enlightened. (65)

The intelligence of one who has not awakened to a loving relationship with the Supreme Divine Person can never find peace. Without peace, where shall one find joy? (66)

Just as a vessel on the sea is pushed by a hurricane, so can a person's intelligence and understanding be battered by the force of sense-desire. (67)

O mighty armed Arjuna, we may conclude that one who has succeeded in subduing the violent force of sense-desire is certainly a sober-minded sage. (68)

What appears as day for enlightened persons seems to be night for conditioned sentient beings, whilst that which appears as daylight for materially conditioned souls seems as the darkness of night to the enlightened ones. (69)

Just as the vast ocean remains steady even though many great rivers flow into it, so a person should remain undisturbed by the continued arising of sense-desires. Such true peace can never be attained by those who are engaged in responding to such desires and acting on their basis. (70)

True peace arises when all sense-desires are transcended and when one acts free from all false conceptions of proprietorship and from the consciousness of exploitation arising from the illusion of one's own supremacy. (71)

Thus I have explained to you the nature of those truly spiritual persons who are never illusioned and who are so fixed in pure consciousness that during the last moments of their earthly sojourn, they are able to consciously enter into their

sacred Homeland, the eternal Realm of the Supreme Divine Person, which is purely spiritual and beyond all suffering.' "
(72)

THE THIRD CHAPTER

Divine Communion
Through Dedicated Service

"Arjuna then said:

'O Master, protector of all the people, You appear to be of the opinion that pure contemplation is superior to active life. Why then do You push me forward into this horrific effort at civil war? (1)

Your words seem inconclusive, and my intellect cannot come into focus unless You affirm more singularly that course of action which will produce the greatest good.' (2)

"The Lord, Who is the reservoir of all beauty, replied:

'O my pure-hearted friend, I have said that in this world there are two types of diligent seekers who come at last to communion with the Supreme – the contemplatives who try to understand the Supreme Truth through the cultivation of scientific theistic knowledge and the persons of action who strive to work with all devotion for the pleasure of the Supreme Person. (3)

By merely abandoning action, a person can neither become purified from the taint of previous misdeeds nor achieve a position transcendental to the laws of action and reaction.

The state of perfection can never be attained through external renunciation alone. (4)

No one can be without engagement, even for an instant, since the quality of nature is that all are forced to act. (5)

Those who attempt to restrict themselves from action on the sensory plane while cherishing the memory of sense-pleasure are hypocrites, and they act through false pretence. (6)

Those who balance the action of the mental and sensual spheres by full engagement of all their faculties in selfless devotional activities are by far more highly evolved. (7)

Rather than yielding to inaction, it is better to perform those actions which are required of you, which are necessary and unavoidable. Without proper engagement even bodily health will deteriorate. (8)

One's endeavours should arise out of a spirit of sacrifice and devotion to the all-pervasive Supreme Divine Person. Action performed for other reasons binds one to the wheel of birth and death. My dear Kaunteya, please perfect within yourself this spirit of acting only for the pleasure of the Supreme, as such a spirit constitutes in itself full liberation. (9)

In primeval times, the Supreme Divine Person, the source of all that lives, having manifested the first of the generations, blessed them and taught them this doctrine of selfless Divine Service. They were told that through the pure endeavour of divine sacrifice they would become wealthy, and all that they could ever possibly desire would come to them. (10)

The *devas*, the subordinate gods who are the empowered controllers of the cosmic functions, being pleased by their devotional efforts would, in turn, please them. Through such divine co-operation, all would gain their fair share of wealth, and blessings of all descriptions would descend upon the land. Working in co-operation and love, everyone would at last come to the Supreme Destination. (11)

The *devas*, seeing such a spirit of self-sacrifice in humanity, naturally provide regular delivery of necessary foodstuffs. On the other hand, those who seek to exploit the gifts of nature without assuming their cosmic responsibilities are no better than thieves. (12)

When foodstuffs are produced in such a devotional way, they have an uplifting and liberating effect on the saints who consume them. But the meals of selfish persons, cooked without thought for others, implicate the eaters in the violence of the food chain, keeping them bound in reaction and guilty of blame. (13)

All living beings require foodstuffs to sustain themselves; and for food, rains are required. When human society is engaged in selfless service, then the rain will not fail to come in proper time and measure. (14)

Selfless action has its roots in the Supreme Divine Person, from Whom the Divine Logos emanates in the living form of the transcendental sound of revealed Truth. Therefore, the all-pervasive Supreme Person may always be communicated with through the selfless performance of the revealed sacrifices. (15)

My dear child of Pritha, those who are satisfied by a superficial life of sense-pleasure, neglecting the Scriptures, waste their valuable human lives. (16)

But those who come to taste the real flavour of their eternal spiritual personalities, who are illumined by awareness of the spirit-self and are fully satisfied by engagement in spiritual activities, transcend all mundane obligations. (17)

Actions should not arise from selfish motives and neither should renunciation. Furthermore, one must never exploit others for one's own gain. (18)

A person who engages continuously in selfless, devotional labours, acting out of spontaneous necessity to render service, achieves the Supreme Destination without fail. (19)

It was through selflessly serving with devotion that great rulers such as Janaka and others came to the plane of perfection. You, also, should give light to the whole world by executing your responsibilities in a similar spirit. (20)

Whatever great and cultured persons do, the general populace runs to imitate. The people naturally follow what they learn from their leaders. (21)

My dear child of Pritha, no action I take anywhere throughout the galaxies is enforced upon Me by duty, and I am in need of nothing, yet still I always go on with My service. (22)

If I ever failed to do what is expected of Me, all humankind would follow in My footsteps. (23)

Were I to falter in My service, the whole world would follow My example and be ruined, and I would be responsible for degradation in the flow of generations. (24)

Persons without information as to the nature of proper action act selfishly and divisively, whereas the truly wise perform their service selflessly with a view to inspire and unite the whole world. (25)

One should not confuse the minds of the unenlightened who are attached to selfish works by encouraging them to become inactive. They must be inspired, instead, to act in devotion. (26)

Souls who allow their false egos to transform them into fools and who are ignorant of the real nature of the self consider themselves to be the cause of their own actions and the results those actions bring. In actual fact, all worldly actions arise on account of the dynamic interweaving of the binding forces of material nature. (27)

A true Master remains always selfless beyond the influence of the binding forces of nature. Such a soul never becomes implicated in the cycle of desire and fulfilment. (28)

Lazy persons who make no effort to cultivate the spirit remain fooled by the magical powers of My external nature and implicated in the reactive chain produced by selfish acts. Nonetheless, the wise should act gently with them. (29)

Rendering your service to Me in consciousness fully illumin-ated by the light of revelation, free from profit motive, put out the fires of nihilism and go forward into battle! (30)

Anyone who acts continuously and selflessly with full faith and devotion to Me and with compassion for all beings is at once free from the cycle of action-reaction. (31)

Those self-centred persons who fail to understand the im-portance of My teachings remain fools despite their so-called learning, and their consciousness is always troubled. (32)

One should try to act in a natural way, for that is the true attainment of the wise. No one can oppose their own nature. (33)

The positive and negative attractions which the sensory objects exercise over the senses are produced by the effects of ancient subtle impressions within the mind-stuff. One must avoid being dominated by such external stimuli, inasmuch as such attachments and aversions represent the major obsta-cles on the path of transcendence. (34)

By adopting a superior conception of action, we are led to conclude that one should follow the law of one's own inner-most being, escaping the temptation to depart from that and follow the path of another. It is better to fail while trying to be oneself than to succeed in becoming someone else.' (35)

"Arjuna then felt inspired to ask:

'O pillar of the Vrishni dynasty, how is it that people sometimes seem forced to blameful actions against their own higher instincts? Even despite their conscious resolution, they appear to be driven just as lifeless things may be driven by wind or water.' (36)

"Lord Krishna, the proprietor of all opulence, replied:

'Self-centred sense-desire, born of the impassioning force of external nature and easily convertible to anger, is the all-destructive, all-entangling Foe in this world. (37)

Each conditioned soul is covered, in some degree, by an element of passionate sense-desire. For some it is like the covering of fire by smoke; for others it is like the coating of a mirror with dust; whilst for others it resembles the enclosure of the embryo within the darkness of the womb. (38)

In this way the soul's pure consciousness is found to be burning in the flames ignited by the Foe, in the form of impassioned sense-desire. (39)

The Foe resides in one's own mind and senses and, from that hiding place, blinds one's inner vision and causes the growth of a myriad of misconceptions. (40)

You are the best amongst the descendants of Bharata, and I therefore implore you to supervise carefully the activities of your senses. Defeat this Foe who has come to eclipse your natural wisdom. (41)

The sensory platform is subordinate to the mental sphere which, in turn, is subordinate to the pure intellect. The position of the spirit-self, however, is still more sublime and powerful. (42)

My mighty-armed friend, it lies with you to conquer this deadly Foe by balancing your mental and intellectual functions with a clearer vision of the transcendent Reality.' " (43)

THE FOURTH CHAPTER

Divine Communion Through Culture of Perfect Understanding

"The omniscient Lord went on:

'In the days long past, I illumined the Deity of the Sun with this understanding. He, in turn, gave instruction to the ancient father of the human race, Manu, who in due course revealed these Truths to Ikshvaku, the founder of the Solar dynasty. (1)

Through the system of preceptorial transmission and apostolic succession, the great and sagacious rulers of society received, understood and passed on the Truth, generation upon generation. As the time went by, however, recollection of humanity's relationship with the Supreme became dimmed and the power of the teaching diminished, my victorious comrade. (2)

Because you love Me and see Me as your friend, I shall this day reveal to you that same scientific understanding which in those very olden days I first transmitted. I shall speak of that mysterious Truth which transcends all darkness.' (3)

"Arjuna then queried:

'You were born a great deal after the Deity of the Sun. How could You have instructed him at the very beginning of the solar system?' (4)

"The ancient and beautiful Lord replied:

'O my noble and heroic friend, You and I have both experienced many lifetimes. I have full recollection of them all, but you are completely unaware of them. (5)

Although for Me there was no birth and My body is not subject to disintegration, and although I am the indwelling controller and master of all sentient beings, nonetheless I am able to manifest to Myself the vision of others through the agency of My own spiritual potencies. (6)

Whenever time and circumstances cause human society to abandon the law of selfless service and, as a result, heinous activities begin to appear, I intervene by manifesting My appearance. (7)

In order to glorify and encourage My saintly devotees, to discipline and reform their persecutors and to establish anew the eternal Truth, I manifest My transcendental pastimes within the world at different times throughout the ages. (8)

Those who understand and show faith in the divine nature of My appearances and pastimes are not forced to take another birth. Instead, my dear friend, they come to dwell with Me. (9)

A great many souls have already come to the stage of taking full shelter in Me, having been purified by penance and the cultivation of perfect understanding. Freed from all false attachments, anxieties and frustrations, they reached the Absolute Reality of My transcendental, loving nature. (10)

I personally reciprocate with every soul who seeks My shelter, and I give Myself to them to the extent they give themselves to Me. My dear child of Pritha, all souls are in reality always on their way to meet Me. (11)

Selfish men seeking success in their profit-oriented actions certainly do well to enlist the aid of the *devas* with whose assistance they will, no doubt, prosper in their worldly civilisation. (12)

You should know that although I am above the process of creation and beyond the influence of change, I am nonetheless the founder of that ancient social system which allows for a natural division of labour between four principal subdivisions of servants on the basis of their qualities and tendencies towards action. (13)

I am never affected by any action and never aspire for fruit from My labours. Those who know Me in truth are also as free as Myself. (14)

In the days of great antiquity, your noble predecessors gained their freedom by acting in this selfless way, and you should now honour those revered forefathers by serving with the same spirit of pure devotion. (15)

I shall explain to you in greater depth this sacred doctrine of Divine Service, which will save you from all inauspicity and bestow full freedom upon your soul. Even the very wise show difficulty in understanding how a life made sacred by active Divine Service excels absolute retirement from effort. (16)

Mystery surrounds the topic of action and makes it difficult to discriminate between actions which are obligatory, those which are prohibited and those which are liberating. (17)

Those persons who understand the liberating effect of active Divine Service and the blame attached to complete retirement from action are distinguished from all humanity as most evolved in intelligence. Such souls remain always close to Me in the midst of all their pious efforts and they fulfil the true purport of all the revealed Scriptures. (18)

The clear-thinking enlightened souls have declared that the fire of perfect understanding is sufficient to destroy all blameful action. Such perfect understanding arises naturally in those who never fix their attention on selfish desires and are sincere in all their attempts. (19)

Such sincere souls never consider their personal profit and always remain self-satisfied with no other centre of interest besides the rendering of loving service to the Supreme Divine Person. They remain completely free no matter what action they perform. (20)

Souls may act to maintain their healthy existence without fear of blame by giving up all false sense of bodily designation and working lovingly with consciousness perfectly centred in the spirit-self. (21)

Be content with that which comes easily; rise above good and evil; culture a pure heart free from envy; be equal in the face of pleasant days and trials. With such an attitude you may act without fear of bondage. (22)

Those who are beyond craving, who are truly free, become illuminated by pure consciousness and their selfless acts in service to the all-pervading Supreme Person, Who is the very soul of action, causing them to become absorbed entirely on the plane of transcendental love. (23)

As cow's ghee is poured as an oblation onto the sacrificial fire, so should the self be offered into the brilliant radiance of a life of Divine Service. Absorption in spiritual activities brings one at once unto the pure spiritual platform. (24)

Amongst spiritually oriented persons, there are some who render first-class service to the *devas* and others who make offerings of prayers and paraphernalia to the sacrificial flame. (25)

There are yet others who engage themselves in constantly hearing transcendental sound vibrations, which allow them to quiet passion, and others still who offer the sensory objects as oblations into the fire of the senses. (26)

Those who desire to be illumined with perfect understanding and to come to the stage of self-mastery should make an offertory out of every action and every breath. (27)

Some saints embrace vows of poverty and absorb themselves in disinterested penance, while others pursue the system of yoga. Another group pursues a course of scriptural research and adheres to rigid vows. (28)

Some are inclined to practise the control of the life-airs, and they become absorbed in trance by restraining first the incoming and then the outgoing breath. Many also regulate their eating habits very strictly while at the same time trying to balance their life-airs. (29)

Although they may appear to be differently engaged, because they are all well-schooled in the art of selfless service, they may all enter, at last, into the immortal region of the spirit where they shall drink the nectar which such sincere service produces. (30)

Selfish souls, on the other hand, will find no peace even in this world, so what will they hope to encounter in the afterlife, O supermost amongst the Kurus? (31)

A wide variety of engagement, arising from the various tendencies towards action, has been approved by the revealed Scriptures, and you may gain your freedom by understanding all of this. (32)

Ever-victorious Arjuna, to make an offering of one's intelligence is considered to be superior to an offering of goods. Offering one's intelligence in Divine Service will bring one perfect understanding, my dear child of Pritha. (33)

All of this knowledge lies in the gentle hands of the genuine Divine Teacher, whom everyone must seek out. If such a wise and holy person is found who has actually gained the vision of Truth and has perfect understanding, as well as the ability to transmit it, then one should make approach with humility, inquire with a sincere heart, render favourable services and request the Master to implant the seed of pure love and theistic devotion in the core of one's heart. (34)

When you have come to know the love of the Supreme Person, you will never again be illusioned. You will see that all living beings are My own children who always remain with Me and are never truly separated from Me, and you will understand in this way that all souls are, in fact, your dear relations. (35)

Even if you be the worst of sinners, when you board the vessel called perfect understanding, you will certainly be able to cross over this sea of troubles. (36)

Just as a blazing bonfire quickly reduces wood to ash, so does the fire of perfect understanding reduce to ash the reactions to all past deeds, my dear Arjuna. (37)

Nothing can be found in this world that can compare to the treasure of perfect understanding, so sublime it is and pure beyond description. Those who culture it, in the maturity of time, become enabled to relish the perfection of their eternal spiritual personalities. (38)

Divine peace and transcendental bliss quickly descend upon the ever-faithful persons who culture perfect understanding and attempt to gain mastery over their sensory demands. (39)

Those who are plagued by misunderstanding show no faith in the Supreme Divine Person or in the sacred teachings. Such souls have no prospect for joy here or in the life hereafter. (40)

O you who are expert in the acquisition of fortune, a soul who remains detached while performing loving service to Me and who eliminates all doubts by development of perfect understanding becomes fully self-realised and completely free from the chain of action-reaction. (41)

Therefore, the misunderstandings that have become lodged in your heart should be driven out with the weapon of perfect understanding. Destroy your doubts and arise, O noble-hearted Bharata; equipped with this doctrine of Divine Service, go on to prevail in the battle!'" (42)

THE FIFTH CHAPTER

Divine Communion Through Genuine Renunciation

"At that time Arjuna inquired of the Lord:

'My dear Krishna, please give me more definitive instructions as to whether it is more beneficial for me to altogether leave the world of action or to take up the sacred path of Divine Service which You have so highly praised.' (1)

"Arjuna's beloved Lord thereupon replied:

'It is no doubt true that both paths may lead in the end to freedom, but I tell you definitely that to act with a spirit of true devotion to the Supreme Person is by far the better course to adopt. (2)

True renunciates never crave for anything and are not repelled by anything. Above the dualities of worldly life, they certainly come to breathe the atmosphere of freedom. (3)

The truly learned assure us that only the less evolved see a fundamental distinction between pure contemplation of the divine phenomena and the practice of Divine Service itself. To follow either path faithfully will ultimately bring one to relish the sweet fruits of them both. (4)

What may be achieved through contemplation may also be attained by the sacred path of service, and thus one who has a clear vision will understand that what seems to be two paths is actually only one. (5)

However, no one who adopts the external garb of a renunciate can hope to gain true joy without engagement in Divine Service. Those saints who become fully absorbed in such purifying service immediately gain communion with the Supreme Truth. (6)

Those who give themselves over entirely to the sacred path of service become established in pristine purity and easily defeat the force of sense-desire. Loving all beings as if they were their very selves, they serve without any fear of adverse effects. (7)

Those who have understood the real truths of life take up the path of Divine Service and never consider themselves to be the final cause of their actions. Seeing, hearing, touching, smelling, eating, moving, sleeping, breathing, talking, giving, receiving, opening and shutting the eyes – they understand all of this to be the mechanical action of the senses in pursuit of their required objects. (8–9)

Just as the leaf of the lotus flower lying upon the pond remains untouched by the water, so the soul who acts in a spirit of full surrender to the Supreme Person remains ever-free from the taint of blame. (10)

The selfless physical, mental and intellectual efforts of those who serve Me with devotion bring about their complete self-purification. (11)

Through dedication to non-fruitive Divine Service, the soul becomes whole and gains lasting peace. The greed of the selfish, on the other hand, is itself a prison. (12)

The body is like a grand house whose eyes, ears, nostrils, mouth and genitive and evacuative organs open out to the world like nine gates. Those who are self-controlled and free from feverish tendencies towards selfish action live a happy life within this house, moving only as the Divine Plan moves them. (13)

The soul, as the house's occupant, can never claim to own the house or to act as the absolute dictator over all its operations, nor should it ever imagine its full produce to be personal profit. It is, after all, by nature that all this goes on. (14)

The all-pervasive Supreme Person is never responsible for one's worldly actions, good or evil, but conditioned souls, illusioned by self-imposed darkness, cannot understand this clearly. (15)

However, upon the rising of the brilliant sun of perfect understanding, one receives the supreme revelation and that darkness is at once naturally dissipated. (16)

Immortality and freedom come quickly to the faithful souls whose hearts have been cleansed of all insecurity by a fully determined and intelligent effort to seek the Divine Shelter. (17)

The hallmark of the truly wise is their gentleness and enlightenment and, especially, their ability to see equally the high-born, refined intellectuals and the low-born, unclean beggars as well as to love even the animals, seeing them all as dear to Me. (18)

Those who can see with such equal vision are free even in this world and display the absolute flawlessness of their jewel-like, pure consciousness. (19)

Being fixed in deep communion with the eternal Supreme Truth, they never become falsely elated by temporal pleasures or depressed by being placed in difficulty. (20)

Due to their connection with the Supreme Beauty, they are always tasting limitless joy and, therefore, easily remain free from the glamour of external attractions. (21)

Misery is born from the womb of selfish, sensual contact, and so the truly enlightened souls never seek pleasure in the exploitation of the sensory world, where everything must know a beginning and an end, my dear Kaunteya. (22)

The only truly happy human beings in this world are those who have overcome the animalistic urges and the force of anger by the power of Divine Grace. (23)

They find their sacred Homeland, the Realm of Supreme Truth, Beauty, Peace and Goodness within their hearts, and their happiness, rejoicing and illumination come from within. (24)

Those who culture a deep inner life totally reintegrate their personalities and begin to serve all life with love. Such souls enter easily the transcendental region which lies beyond all sufferings. (25)

Free from the force of sense-desire and its companion, anger, the divine servants who have mastered the truth of conscious life enter that sacred Abode of perfect consciousness very quickly. (26)

Those who wish to envision this Realm of transcendental bliss within should detach themselves from the 'stage set' world and concentrate on balancing the life-airs and penetrating the spirit-centre situated just above the nose between the eyebrows. Such practice will bring calm to the senses, the mind and the intellect, and will empower one to cast off selfish desires, unfounded fears and self-destructive anger. Those who succeed in this are certain to taste full freedom. (27–28)

I am the proper beneficiary of all the sacred acts of sacrifice, and it is I Whom people hope to please through penance. It is I alone Who am the true Lord of all the galaxies and the King of Kings! I truly am the ever well-wishing friend of every soul. It is only by such understanding that a person can become whole and that the world can attain peace.' " (29)

THE SIXTH CHAPTER

Divine Communion Through Prayer and Contemplation

"The all-knowing Lord continued:

'Those who serve out of a sense of sacred obligation and not out of a desire for payment are genuine renunciates, sincere seekers of Truth. However, this cannot be said of those who culture complete inaction and will undergo no sacrifice for My sake. (1)

No one can come to know full communion with Me without first turning away from mental cravings. Genuine renunciation is a fundamental characteristic of pure devotional service. (2)

For those who are novices on the way towards communion with Me, active engagement in the purifying practice of Divine Service is said to be the means for attaining perfection. Those perfect servants who have already attained to deep communion with Me are seen to be ever tranquil and blessed. (3)

A person may be said to be in full communion with Me when the tendency to respond slavishly to mental stimuli has been overcome, when self-motivated action has been given up and sensory demands transcended. (4)

One must consciously arrange for one's deliverance and not unconsciously fall into degradation. The mind may either act as our great ally or our deadly enemy. (5)

For those who have achieved self-mastery, the mind is like a pleasant friend, but those who have failed to do so appear to be living with a treacherous enemy. Indeed, they become enemies to their very selves. (6)

The fully realised souls, having attained the summit of self-mastery, live in deep communion with the Supreme Person, caring not for heat and cold, happiness and misery, prestige or disrepute. (7)

Self-satisfied with the attainment of the divine wisdom which comes through self-mastery, absorbed in the sublime and precious Truth, the saints see gold to be no different from stone. (8)

Those who are far advanced naturally show love to both saints and sinners, wish well to both friends and foes, and seek to act as peacemakers amongst the belligerents. (9)

Those who seek such perfection should retire to a secluded place for prayer and become absorbed in continuous devotion, carefully guarding the consciousness to keep it free from false attractions and exploitative tendencies. (10)

Having found an appropriate sitting place in some pure and holy land, they should sit comfortably, after first laying down a grass mat and a cloth, and then with single-pointed attention they should balance the mind, absorb the consciousness and, in this way, purify the heart. (11–12)

Keeping their bodies straight with heads erect, they should remain still and free the eyes from distraction. With peaceful and happy minds, undisturbed by fears, firmly continent and resolved, they should absorb full consciousness in Me, making Me the ultimate goal of life. (13–14)

The saints who constantly practise in this way quickly make friendship with their minds, come to taste the peace that lies beyond all suffering, and finally come to live with Me. (15)

Communion with Me can best be maintained by those who neither eat nor fast to excess, sleep to excess, or too often keep a night vigil. (16)

The middle way should be followed in matters of diet, exercise, work and rest, as such practice will help one to overcome all suffering. (17)

Those souls who have learned to discipline consciousness and remain fixed in transcendence, beyond the force of sense-desire, may be said to be true adepts. (18)

Just as a flame sheltered from the breeze burns bright and steady, so shines the consciousness of the saints absorbed in full communion with Me. (19)

Arriving at the plane of pure consciousness, wherein the practice of Divine Service has brought about self-restraint, they gain a position to relish the complete satisfaction which comes from seeing the true self. (20)

Solidly reposed in the Supreme Truth, their connection with the universe comes through transcendental senses, through which they taste infinite pleasure and a holy joy. (21)

Upon reaching such a platform, the self-realised souls conclude that there remain no more goals worthy of achievement. Being so deeply absorbed in Divine Communion, they know no agitation, even in the face of severe difficulties. Such steady absorption in Divine Service should be understood as the only remedy for the miseries which arise from mundane connection. (22–23)

Divine Service should be practised with confidence and in a clear consciousness of communion with Me. Completely transcending the force of the sense-desires generated by mental stimuli, one should use the mind as a regulator over the sensory movement. (24)

Progress should be gradual, stage-by-stage, and full conviction must be achieved by reasoned intelligence. At last the mind will always graze in the pasturing grounds of the eternal Homeland, the Realm of Supreme Truth and Beauty, and will never wander elsewhere. (25)

Wherever the mind wanders through impetuosity and intemperate habit, it must certainly be brought back and placed under the shelter of the Divine Herdsman. (26)

By absorbing their minds in full consciousness of Me, My divine servants experience transcendental pleasure of the highest order. With passions calmed, they achieve freedom from blame and come to perceive the Supreme Divine Person face to face. (27)

By continuous engagement on the sacred path of service, the self-realised souls are completely cleansed of all worldly pollution, and coming to know the Supreme Truth personally, they relish the highest ambrosia of divine life. (28)

Souls in full communion with Me see Me seated in the hearts of all and realise that all souls also dwell in My heart. True saints cannot help but see Me everywhere. (29)

Those who perceive My presence in all places and see all things in relationship to Me are never deprived of My shelter, nor ever forgotten by Me. (30)

My divine servants see in truth that I am the One Who dwells within the hearts of all, and thus they remain fully devoted to Me in all circumstances. True saints love all souls as if they were their very selves and understand their joys and sorrows.' (31–32)

"Arjuna then responded:

'O destroyer of the demons of doubt, the path towards Divine Communion which You have pointed out appears to be beyond the power of my restless and flickering mind to follow, for the mind is indisputably unstable, easily agitated, powerful and obdurate. My dear Krishna, I think it would be easier to calm a gale than to tame it.' (33–34)

"The Blessed Lord thereupon replied:

'There is no doubt, my mighty-armed Kaunteya, that it is very hard to bring tranquillity to the stormy mind, but success will come in the end by continuous practice and total dedication. (35)

Failure to tame the mind will place communion with Me out of reach, but it is My conviction that those who learn to properly supervise the mind's activities by adopting appropriate spiritual techniques are certain to achieve success.' (36)

"Then Arjuna asked:

'What becomes of a faithful soul who, after taking up the divine way, allows the mind to be deviated, and thus fails to achieve the perfection of Divine Communion? (37)

Does not such a person lose everything like a cloud when it bursts, having no more a place in this world and yet unable to follow the road laid down by the Supreme Person? Such souls have turned their backs on material success, but have no hope for liberation. (38)

This is my uncertainty, and I beg You to do away with it entirely. I shall find no one apart from You, my dear Krishna, Who has the power to resolve this doubt, because You alone are all-knowing.' (39)

"The all-attractive Lord then said:

'My dear child of Pritha, those who take up the path of auspicious action shall never come to an evil destination, either in this world or in the hereafter. Goodness can only beget goodness. (40)

Deviated from the purely spiritual path, the immature aspirants will enter the subtle planes of celestial enjoyment, which are populated by devout souls who have performed volumes of pious deeds. After many years there, they will again take birth in happy families of holy and aristocratic parents. (41)

Alternatively, they may be fortunate enough to take birth in a family of My devoted servants, who are always enthused by love for Me. A birth such as this is a rare and precious opportunity. (42)

Having gained such a favourable birth, their consciousness of Divine Service is reawakened and, taking up from where they left off, they strive again to reach the perfection of love, O valiant son of the Kurus. (43)

By dint of prenatal experience, they are drawn intuitively to inquire about the way of Divine Communion, and they quickly rise above the detailed injunctions of the Scriptures. (44)

Those who sincerely endeavour attain a consciousness purified of all pollution and, because of the efforts of their many previous births, they are able to quickly achieve the highest goal of life. (45)

Those who seek communion with Me are of higher order than the ascetics, the scholars and the selfish workers. You must therefore always strive for such Divine Communion, my beloved Arjuna. (46)

It is My conviction that of all those who seek Me, those ever-faithful souls who always live in love with Me, continuously seeing Me in the core of their hearts and always worshipping Me by engagement in selfless Divine Service, attain to the deepest levels of communion with Me and are the best amongst all souls.' " (47)

THE SEVENTH CHAPTER

Divine Communion Through Developed Spiritual Intelligence

"The Lord of all opulence then said:

'By hearing carefully from Me with your mind and heart fully attached to Me, you will experience Divine Communion in My shelter and be entirely freed from all misgivings and doubts. (1)

I shall give you a full explanation of both the manifest universe and the divine mysteries underlying creation. Understanding all of this, you will find that there remains nothing unknown in all the worlds. (2)

Within human society, only one out of thousands seeks self-perfection, and even amongst those who have reached perfection, hardly any know Me as I truly am. (3)

My insentient nature is comprised of eight divisions – the earthen, the aqueous, the fiery and radiant, the airy, the ethereal, the mental, the intellectual and the veil of false ego which covers the real identity of the self. (4)

In addition to this insentient nature, you should understand that I have a higher nature as well, which is comprised of the living souls who utilise the resources of the world, inhabiting bodies made of its substance. (5)

I am the unitary source of all consciousness, time, space, energy and mass. By Me the world is manifested and at its end dissolved. (6)

O achiever of great affluence, My existence is the highest and most fundamental of Truths, the underlying basis for all and for everything, like the thread which draws together a strand of pearls. (7)

I am the flavour of pure water, the light of moons and suns, the sacred syllable AUM in the Holy Scriptures, the sound transported through space, and all that which is truly human in humankind. (8)

I am the pleasing fragrance of the earth, the warm radiance of the fire, the life of all sentient beings and the self-sacrifice of the austere. (9)

Please try to understand, my dear child of Pritha, that I am the originating seed of all organic life, the illumination that brightens the intellect of the wise, and the fortitude which strengthens the hearts of great heroes. (10)

I am the great potency of those powerful souls whose passions and attachments are gone, and that sexual union which does not contravene the laws of love and virtue. (11)

All manifestations – the harmonious, the energetic and the inertial – evolve from Me alone and I am, therefore, the sum and substance of all, yet I nonetheless remain independent of all creation. (12)

The entirety of the universal creation remains illusioned by the spell of the diverse forces of material manifestation and, therefore, cannot understand Me, for I am transcendental to the world, imperishable and without limits. (13)

The divine and magical forces of My material nature are like tight ropes from which it is difficult to become unbound, but those who lovingly take shelter of Me easily escape from this illusory bondage. (14)

However, it is not given to foolish evil-doers to take loving shelter of Me. Those of atheistic nature, whose intelligence is overshadowed by darkness and illusion, are the lowest amongst humankind. (15)

O most worthy amongst the descendants of Bharata, four types of pious souls serve Me with devotion – the suffering in want of healing, the seekers in search of Truth, the needy in quest for riches, and the wise in pursuit of the Absolute Reality. (16)

Amongst all of them, those enlightened souls who have come to communion with Me by possessing exclusive and loving devotion to Me are super-excellent; so dear am I to them and they to Me. (17)

Noble indeed are all the enlightened souls, but those who possess a perfect understanding of their eternal relationship of love with Me are just like My very self. By serving Me with devotion, they arrive at the unparalleled goal, the sacred Homeland, the Realm of the Supreme Divine Person. (18)

At the end of many incarnations, the enlightened souls take loving shelter of Me, understanding Me to be the source and substance of all that is. Such highly evolved souls are very rare and precious. (19)

Those whose understanding is obscured by mental cravings take shelter of a pantheon of other gods and, being bound by their natures, undertake to worship them by appropriate means. (20)

It is I Who make stable the faith of those who choose to worship these lesser and subordinate gods, wishing to satisfy temporal desires. (21)

Those who possess such faith worship these subordinate deities and have their desires satisfied, but in fact I alone oversee the bestowal of all such benedictions. (22)

Persons of less-developed consciousness achieve the perishable rewards which they seek. Pleasing the gods, they go to dwell with them for a while in paradise, but those who worship Me attain everlasting life with Me. (23)

Those whose wisdom is not yet fully evolved think that My form and personality are a product of the impersonal and unmanifested Absolute. They have failed to penetrate to an understanding of My personal existence, which is imperishable and beyond all limits. (24)

I reserve the right to remain invisible to the faithless, whose eyes I keep covered by the magic of My divine potency. In this way the world remains ignorant of the fact that I am the beginningless and inexhaustible source of all existences. (25)

I am equally aware of past, present and future, and I know every soul very well, my dear Arjuna, yet I remain unknown. (26)

Deluded by the world's dualities and overcome by cravings and hatred, all the souls in this world remain in ignorance, O conqueror of the foes. (27)

However, those virtuous souls whose blameful actions are at an end become liberated from all illusion by serving Me with loving devotion and determined vows. (28)

Seeking freedom from old age and death, such undeluded souls come to take shelter of Me by rendering loving service, and in this way they gain an understanding of the complete spectrum of transcendental and fruitive actions. (29)

The fully awake consciousness of those who know Me as the Supreme Divine Person, the force within the atom, the source of all the godly overlords, and the supreme indwelling spirit within all hearts, can remain in a complete awareness of Me, which is uninterrupted even at the time of their death.' " (30)

THE EIGHTH CHAPTER

The Nature of the Immortal Spirit

"Arjuna inquired:

'How may spirit be defined, and what is the true nature of the eternal spiritual personality or soul? What constitutes reactive action? O most excellent of all personalities, what is the regulating principle within mundane existence, and from where do the *devas* derive their power? (1)

How does the Supreme Divine Person, Who hears our prayers and accepts our offerings, live within our bodies? Finally, how may those who have gained self-mastery come to perceive and understand You at the time they leave their mortal frames?' (2)

"The Lord then replied:

'By spirit we mean the immaterial, imperishable, pure and transcendental living divine substance of which each individual and eternal sentient being is constituted. It is this immortal self which is the true self, the eternal spiritual personality. Movement based on specific desire brings about the manifestation of the varied external forms, which the self identifies with in this world, and such movement is called reactive action. (3)

The basic principle of atomic structure and of organic existence is endless change. I, Myself, in the form of cosmic energy, am the all-pervasive creative intelligence which manifests and governs the universes, and the *devas* – the godly regulators who control the universal functions – derive their power from Me. It is I Who listen to the prayers of all, I for Whom all the offerings of sacrifice are made, and I Who am the supreme spirit living as a friend within the hearts of all embodied souls. (4)

If one's consciousness is filled with remembrance of Me at the last moments of one's life within the body, then one is sure to reach Me. Have no doubt of this. (5)

Whatever state of consciousness one is in at the end of a lifetime will determine the state of being which the soul will experience after disconnection with the body. (6)

You should, therefore, remember Me at every moment and, at the same time, strive to carry out your duty. Dedicating your heart and mind to Me, you can rest assured that you will come to Me. (7)

Anyone who makes a conscious practice of communing with Me, always chastely thinking of Me, arrives before long in My divine and transcendental Abode, my dear child of Pritha. (8)

One should contemplate always upon the original Poet, the all-knowing Author of the cosmos, the most ancient and sovereign Ruler of all creation, Who is more fundamental than the atom, the sustenance of all existences, far beyond all limited conceptions, with a transcendental form so beautiful as to give illumination to the sun. (9)

One who remains established powerfully in conscious communion with the Supreme Person, with a heart filled with devotion, will be able to fix the air of life in the spirit-centre between the two eyebrows and be transported from there to My personal presence in the transcendental, divine Realm. (10)

Now I shall speak briefly of the supreme goal of life, the inexhaustible Reservoir of Truth, Whom the erudite scholars of Holy Scripture seek to know, Whom the devout hermits hope to meet in the wilderness, and Whom the students of spiritual life inquire after. (11)

Divine Communion may be brought about by carefully reglating all the media of perception, focusing the mind upon one's heart of hearts, and allowing the air of life to rise up to the crown of one's head. (12)

Thus established in contemplative trance, one should vibrate the primordial sound, the sacred syllable AUM, while remaining established in remembrance of Me. If one leaves the body in such consciousness, then the transcendental world will assuredly be reached. (13)

In fact, for those who remember Me always, never allowing a gap in their devotion, I am very easily attainable. (14)

Having achieved supreme perfection, the most exalted of souls never again are forced to take birth within the temporal world, the domain of suffering. (15)

On all the planets within the universe where there is life, the sufferings of continual birth and death go on, but those who have reached the planets of My Divine Realm achieve everlasting life with Me. (16)

A thousand millenniums passing in this world represent one day in the life of the universal creation, and another thousand passing are as its night. Thus should humanity understand the relativity of time. (17)

Through the billions of years of each 'day', the infinity of beings act out their dreams on the stage of the world, but when the 'night' comes, they remain as if asleep with their consciousness unmanifest. (18)

Day after day dawns and again all souls awake, but as soon as nightfall comes, they all lapse into unconsciousness. (19)

There is, however, an everlasting existence which is transcendental to the material flux and which remains intact even at the dissolution of the mundane world. (20)

In the imperishable world that lies beyond all mundane manifestation, I maintain My eternal residence, and those fortunate souls who have realised their supreme destiny reach Me there and are never forced to return to the worlds of birth and death. (21)

Continuous and exclusive devotional love is the only means by which the super-excellence of the Supreme Person may be realised. Present in every atom of the universal creation, all existences are but expansions of the various potencies of that Supreme Energetic Source. (22)

O most worthy descendent of King Bharata, the mystics show concern that they may leave their bodies at a time conducive to their final release from rebirth. I shall explain this matter to you now. (23)

Those persons who possess deep spiritual understanding leave their bodies during the period after the time of the winter solstice but before the summer comes, at an auspicious moment during the bright fortnight of the moon, in the daytime and in the presence of fire and light. (24)

The mystics who leave the world at night during the dark fortnight of the moon, after the summer solstice but before the winter comes, and in the presence of smoke, enter the effulgence of the moon to drink nectar, but have to return to this world again. (25)

In the opinion of the Holy Scriptures, one may pass from this world in light or in darkness. Those who leave their bodies in light never return to the world, whereas those who leave in darkness must return. (26)

Although it is very well that you know this, in actual fact, My devotees need never be concerned about the details of these different paths. Therefore, my dear Arjuna, you should simply always remain absorbed in deep and loving communion with Me. (27)

Those who worship Me with devotion arrive at the natural condition of supreme peace and blissfulness in My sacred, spiritual Realm, and thus achieve more than can be gained through performance of elaborate and costly sacrifices, voluntary acceptance of austerity, liberal giving in charity and other such pious works.' " (28)

THE NINTH CHAPTER

The Royal Science
of the Mysteries
# of Divine Communion

"The all-merciful Lord then said:

'Because you have an innocent heart, I shall disclose to you that secret path of wisdom which, having been fully realised, will lead you to complete freedom from suffering. (1)

This most royal of sciences is the supreme monarch amongst mysteries, the purest and most holy of ways. It brings one to the direct perception of the spiritual Realm, which should be understood as the final accomplishment of all religions, and it bestows supreme joy which lasts forever. (2)

Those who are without sincere faith in the path of loving devotion can never reach Me. They face continued rebirth amidst the obstructions and harassments of the mundane world and must continually experience death. (3)

I am ever-present at every locale throughout creation in a form invisible to mundane eyes. All sentient beings have their existence in My existence, yet I am never dependent on them. (4)

It is only indirectly, through the agency of My inconceivable divine potencies, that I give sustenance to those living in this world and provide a foundation for the cosmos. Nevertheless, it is I, Myself, Who am the unitary source of all existences. (5)

Just as the breezes blow freely, floating in the sky, so you should understand that all living entities are floating within the vast ocean of My existence. (6)

O most dear son of Kunti, at the conclusion of each universal time cycle, all sentient beings, as well as the manifested material nature, are absorbed into Me. And at the dawn of the next cycle, I again manifest the varied creation through the expansion of My potencies. (7)

I am the proprietor of the material nature, and when My potent will enters into it, the diverse phenomena of the unversal order become manifest. By My will this occurs time and time again. (8)

This work of creation cannot bind Me, because I maintain a position of neutrality and hold no special attachment to any aspect of creation. (9)

Material nature manifests all animate and inanimate existences under My supervision, and all mundane phenomena may be ultimately traced to this cause. (10)

Because I appear in human form, the ignorant think low of Me, assuming Me to be an ordinary person. They are unable to understand the supreme nature of My existence or My sovereignty over all creation. (11)

Persons of atheistic temperament who do not hesitate to do evil remain bewildered as if under a magic spell. They lose all hope, become frustrated in all their plan-making, and are simply baffled by their scientific efforts to gain knowledge. (12)

The most highly evolved of souls take direct shelter of My divine nature and absorb themselves fully on the sacred path of service, never allowing themselves to be distracted from remembering Me as the inexhaustible fountainhead of all creation. (13)

Such noble and sublime persons may always be seen to be singing My praises, attempting with determined effort to please Me, offering their humble respects to Me within the temples and within the hearts of all, and perpetually absorbed in the rapture of pure devotional ecstasy. (14)

There are other souls who by culture of spiritual understanding offer homage to Me, and still others who seek an undifferentiated oneness with Me. Some see the diversities of the world and worship My various potencies, whereas others hold a pantheistic view and are unable to see past My cosmic form. (15)

It is I Who am the ceremony at which the Soma beverage is consecrated and I Who am the very essence of the offering of sacrifice to God. I am the curative potency of all the healing herbs, the source of power and deliverance in the sacred chants and psalms, the fire of sacrifice and the melted butter thrown into it as oblation. (16)

I am the father and the mother of the universe; indeed, I am its grandfather and the very root of its existence. I am the entirety of all that is to be understood, I purify all that comes into contact with Me, and I am Myself the sacred sound AUM and the Rig, Sama and Yajur Vedas. (17)

I am the supreme goal of life, the sustenance of all, the greatest master, the ever-present witness, the true home of everyone, the only safe shelter and the most sincere friend. In Me the universe has its primeval origins and in Me it will have its end. I am the limitless ground upon which everything rests and the seed from which everything was born. (18)

My dear Arjuna, I provide heat to the world and it is I Who send forth the rains. I provide the nectar of life everlasting, yet I am also the Lord of death. Both the eternal and the temporal come from Me. (19)

The process of Vedic sacrifice at which the Soma beverage is consumed is described in the three Vedas as having the potency to cleanse one of all sin. Some Vedic scholars, therefore, carry out these sacrifices with a view towards gaining access to celestial paradises and enjoying the opulent pleasures of the gods. (20)

Having relished such great pleasures in the celestial realms, they must again return to this world and live under the shadow of death when the credits they have earned through their self-interested sacrifice have all been spent. Thus, their study of the doctrines of the Holy Scriptures gains them only temporal happiness, because their desire is selfish. (21)

However, I come personally to meet the every requirement and insure the full security of those who are undeviating in their remembrance of Me and perpetually absorbed in a consciousness of pure devotion. (22)

Plagued with misunderstanding, souls offer faithful homage to other gods, yet all their offerings are really intended for Me only. (23)

For I am the true enjoyer at all the sacrifices and, indeed, I am their governing principle. Those who do not know this truth about Me are out of touch with the Absolute Reality. (24)

Those who worship the *devas* take birth in their company; those who carry out ancestor worship go to be with their forefathers; those who worship ghosts and evil spirits find their place with such creatures; but those who follow the sacred path of My Divine Service come to live with Me personally. (25)

I come Myself to accept the love-saturated offerings of My pure devotees, even if they be a simple leaf, a flower, a fruit or a little water. (26)

My dear Kaunteya, whatever you eat and drink, whatever you offer in sacrifice or give away in charity, and whatever penance you perform, let it all be done with love as an offering to Me. (27)

You will thereby become liberated, even in this life, from both favourable and unfavourable reactions, and will become free from the bondage to fruitive work. By establishing your consciousness in loving communion with Me, you will gain the complete freedom that comes with My personal presence. (28)

I am equally disposed towards all sentient beings, having no rivals and playing no favourites. Yet for those who offer their loving service to Me with hearts filled with devotion, I become personally present. (29)

Persons of saintly character who engage uninterruptedly in My divine, loving service must be considered to be completely pure, even if by chance they appear to perform some impure act. (30)

After a very short time, they become fully reconciled with Divine Law and achieve enduring peace. My dear Kaunteya, you should openly proclaim that My pure devotees shall never be failures. (31)

Anyone who follows the path of surrender to Me is certain to achieve the supreme goal of life, be they low-born or high, male or female, wealthy merchants or simple labourers. (32)

How exalted then are the great teachers, the pious devotees and the sagacious monarchs who, in the midst of this temporal and unhappy world, remain fully absorbed in loving service to Me. (33)

Always absorb your mind in remembering Me, remain lovingly devoted to Me, adore Me with your acts of worship and humbly kneel down before Me. Entering into such complete Divine Communion, you will surely reach My personal presence.' " (34).

THE TENTH CHAPTER

The Glorious Perfection
of the Supreme Person

"The Master of all mystic beauty, Lord Krishna, then said:

'Please hear from Me carefully as I describe to you again the glories of the Supreme Divine Person. I speak out of a deep affection for you and a great concern for your welfare. (1)

The source of My existence cannot be fathomed even by the most powerful of beings or the most exalted of wise men, because I am, in fact, the fountainhead from which all such persons spring. (2)

Those who understand Me to be the birthless, primordial Sovereign of the cosmos are beyond illusion, and their hearts are washed clean of all that misunderstanding which causes blameful actions and leads to death. (3)

All of the various qualities of consciousness which the souls who reside in this world display have their source in Me. These include the intellect, with its power to investigate and perform self-analysis, as well as the faculty of discrimination, through which matter and spirit may be differentiated. The ethical capacity that allows one to forgive the transgressions of others and to distinguish between truth and falsity comes from Me, as does the power to restrain the senses from the pursuit of their objects, to focus inner perception and to contemplate upon Supreme Truth. From Me comes sensitivity to pleasure and pain and the instincts which guide one through the processes of being born and of dying. Feelings of fear and anxiety as well as their relief, sentiments of compassion for others, the sense of self-contentment, the capacity for doing penance and practising altruism, and the awareness of good and evil repute – all of these have their origin in Me. (4–5)

The great ancestors of the people of this world, the sages and the progenitors, were all born from the power of My mind. (6)

Gaining an understanding of the truths concerning My divine opulences and supernatural potencies will lead one to become perfectly established in loving communion with Me through selfless Divine Service. There is certainly no doubt of this. (7)

I am the unitary source from Whom all of the power in the universe is generated, and all creation emanates from Me. The truly wise understand this and become devoted to Me in love. (8)

The consciousness of saintly persons is always absorbed in ecstatic love for Me, and all of their life energy is dedicated to My service. When in the company of like-minded souls, they take great relish in discussing theistic topics, and to humanity at large they make an effort to spread Divine Love.

In this way, they live a life of the greatest pleasure and satisfaction. (9)

Unto all those who are perpetually engaged in the ecstasy of offering loving service to Me, I bestow the enlightened understanding that will bring them to perfect intimacy with Me. (10)

Desiring to shower My blessings upon them and to eradicate all misunderstanding, I, from My position within, illuminate their heart of hearts with the radiant torchlight of transcendental awareness.' (11)

"Arjuna then responded as follows:

'O my Lord, You are the Supreme Divine Person, the ultimate place of pilgrimage and shelter, totally pure and perfect. You are the original Personality of transcendence, the primeval Lord of all creation, without birth and without limits. All who are great in wisdom, sages like the divine Narada, Asita, Devala and the learned Vyasa, have given testimony of this, and now You are confirming it with Your own witness. (12–13)

O Krishna, O Keshava, I believe that all Your words are Absolute Truth. The revelation of Your position as the all-attractive Supreme Person, the reservoir of all opulences, is understood by neither the pious nor the powerful. (14)

In fact, You are incomprehensible to all but Yourself for You alone are equipped with sufficient potency to understand Your own glories. You are indeed the source of all that be, sovereign Emperor of the galaxies, Lord of Lords and Master of the entire cosmic creation! (15)

I would like to hear from You a more specific and complete description of the opulent and perfect transcendental potencies, by which You permeate all existence with Your presence. (16)

O Supreme Goal of all the saintly mystics, please tell me how I may keep my consciousness always absorbed in You and in what way I should contemplate upon Your all-attractive divine forms. (17)

Please go on describing the amazing extent of Your mystic power and beauty, for my ears are never satiated by the flow of nectar from Your lips, O shelter of all the people!' (18)

"The Blessed Lord then said:

'I shall certainly be pleased to speak further about My divine character but, in doing so, I shall have to point out only the principal amongst My personal opulences, which in fact are infinite in their scope, O great chief of the Kuru dynasty. (19)

I am the very soul of everything and am situated within the hearts of all. I am the origin, the support and the destination of every sentient being, My dear Arjuna. (20)

Amongst godly figures, I am Vishnu, the all-pervasive One. Of luminous things, I am the radiant and life-giving sun. I am Marichi amongst the gods of outer space, and of all the stars, I am the soothing moon. (21)

Amongst the Holy Scriptures, I am the hymns of the Sama Veda, and amongst the celestial overlords, I am Indra, the King of paradise. Of all the sensory faculties, I am the mind, and I am the force of conscious life within the living. (22)

Amongst the powers of destruction, I am Shankara, the great Lord Shiva, and of the powerful, subtle beings, I am Kuvera, the chief treasurer of the gods. Within the family of the Vasus, I am the deity of the fire, and of mighty mountains, I am Mount Meru at the universal centre. (23)

You should understand, My dear child of Pritha, that of high priests, I am the most eminent, Brihaspati. Of warlords, I am Generalissimo Kartikeya, the son of Lord Shiva, and of seas, I am the mighty ocean. (24)

Amongst great seers of the Truth, I am the sage Bhrigu. Amongst all words and sounds, I am the imperishable syllable AUM. Of all forms of divine sacrifice, I am the recitation of the Holy Names of God, and of stationary objects, I am the range of Himalayas. (25)

Amongst great trees, I am the sacred fig tree. Of godly sages, I am Narada Muni. Of those with clear voices who sing for the pleasure of the gods, I am Chitraratha, and of all perfected souls, I am the wise Kapila. (26)

Of horses, I am Uccaihshrava, who was produced along with the elixir of immortality when the gods and demons churned the ocean. Of mighty elephants, I am Airavata, who was also produced from nectar, and in human society, I am that monarch who gives light to the people. (27)

Amongst weapons, I am the Vajra, the cosmic thunderbolt, and of cows, I am Kamadhenu, that miraculous bovine whose udders yield the fruits of all desires. Of those who beget children, I am Cupid, the god of sexual love, and amongst the snake community, I am the pious Vasuki. (28)

Of cosmic serpents, I am Ananta, possessed of limitless heads, and of all those who live beneath the water, I am the resident monarch, Varuna. Amongst the forefathers of humankind, I am Aryama, who presides over the planets of the ancestors, and of all those who regulate the affairs of the world, I am Yama, who oversees death and transmigration. (29)

Within the midst of the family of demons descending from Diti, I am the saintly Prahlada, and amongst all conquerors, I am time, which conquers all. Amongst the beasts of the jungle, I am the lordly lion, and of all the many different birds, I am Garuda, who carries Narayana and Lakshmi upon his back. (30)

Of all that purifies, I am the wind, and amongst those who are expert in the use of weaponry, I am the great King Rama. Amongst aquatics, I am the shark, and of streams of flowing water, I am the beautiful Jahnavi, the sacred Ganges. (31)

I am the beginning, middle and end of all creation, my dear Arjuna. Amongst forms of education, I am that science which leads to perfect knowledge of the self, and in an argument, I am the natural and logical conclusion. (32)

In the alphabet, I am the first letter A, and of different types of words, I am the dual compound. I am the eternal feature of time and the Lord of creative potency, whose many faces point in all directions. (33)

I am death, which consumes all, and I am the source of all that which has not yet come to be. Amongst women, I am the presiding goddesses of the perfect feminine qualities: good reputation, beauty and opulence, sharp memory, deep intelligence, steadfastness in service, and patient forgiveness. (34)

Of songs, I am the beautiful Brihati hymn sung to the Lord at midnight, and of all poetic verses, I am the transcendental rhythm of the Gayatri invocation. Of months, I am the months of harvest, and of seasons, I am the fragrant days of spring. (35)

Amongst frauds, I am the cheating gambler, and of all that which is radiant, I am the radiance. I am the sense of victory in all winners, the spirit of adventure in the brave, and the goodness of all those who are good and true. (36)

Within the Vrishni dynasty, I am the son of Vasudev, and within the family of Pandu, I am Arjuna. Of all the learned philosophers, I am Vyasa, the compiler of the Vedas, and of deep thinkers, I am Shukra, the professor of the unsurrendered souls. (37)

Amongst those who must keep order, I am the penalties which they impose upon the lawless, and of those who seek after success, I am those who keep to righteous means. Of those things which must be kept secret, I am the protecting vow of silence, and I am the wisdom possessed by the wise. (38)

My dear Arjuna, I am the seed from which all living things grow up, and nothing, animate or inanimate, could exist if I did not exist. (39)

Infinite indeed are My opulences and potencies, O hero amongst men, and the examples that I have given you are by no means complete. (40)

You should understand that all that is substantial, beautiful and glorious within creation is born from a tiny fragment of My lustrous majesty. (41)

So what will you gain by knowing all these varied things? It is enough to know that, indeed, I AM, and that with a single spark of My mystic nature I uphold and pervade the entire cosmos.' " (42)

THE ELEVENTH CHAPTER

The Vision of Lord Krishna's Cosmic Form

"Arjuna then said:

'You have shown great kindness to me by revealing matters so high, so confidential and of such great spiritual import. Your words have been so illuminating that my illusions have all been dissipated. (1)

O my lotus-eyed Lord, I have listened with care to Your delineation of the metaphysical evolution and destiny of the living souls and to Your account of the inconceivable and glorious nature of Your divine qualities. (2)

Although I understand that this form which I see before me is actually the form of the Supreme Person, I nonetheless desire to see Your fully majestic cosmic form, O chief executive of the universes! (3)

O my Master, most powerful of mystics, if, in Your opinion, I am qualified to see Your form of infinite power, then please reveal it to me.' (4)

"The Lord, Who is the form of infinite opulence, then said:

'My dear Arjuna, awaken your inner vision to observe hundreds of thousands of diverse forms coloured in all the pigments of the rainbow. (5)

Observe first-hand all the varied figures of the *devas*, the glowing bodies of the sons of light, the potent controller of destruction, the powers which generate healing, the controllers of the winds and fire, and a multitude of other amazing and wonderful things that no one has been privileged to see before. (6)

O Arjuna, My dear and enlightened friend, I give you now the vision to be able to see all the animate and inanimate phenomena of the entire cosmic creation, compressed into a single unitary design. Behold therein whatever it is that you may like to see. (7)

You would never have been able to see this visionary display of My majestic and mystical potencies with your normal eyes, and I have therefore bestowed upon you divine eyes which are equipped to see the super-mundane.'" (8)

Sanjaya, who was relaying the report of the Lord's encounter with Arjuna to his monarch, Dhritarashtra, then gave the following description:

"O my royal-blooded Sire, while speaking in this way, Lord Krishna, the deliverer of the world and the supreme proprietor of all miraculous powers, revealed to the son of

Queen Kunti His super-excellently majestic and opulent cosmic form. (9)

How wonderful is the vision of this form of infinite radiance, possessed of the power to permeate all of cosmic creation! Within it are an infinity of divine faces and figures, all ornamented with jewellery of exquisite design and craftsmanship, clothed in mystic splendour, garlanded with celestial flowers, equipped with magic swords and bows, and anointed with the most fragrant of divine perfumes. (10–11)

If all at once untold thousands of suns were to appear in the sky, their brilliant light would only faintly approximate the splendour of this cosmic feature of the Almighty Supreme Divine Person. (12)

This vision of all the diverse profusion of universal phenomena, assembled in a unitary divine figure, streamed in on the son of Pandu by the grace of the Lord of Lords. (13)

Folding his hands together in prayer and bowing down his head in humility before the Lord, Arjuna, who was overcome with the wondrous nature of the vision and whose body was thrilled with divine ecstasy, then began to address his Master in the following words:

'O Almighty Lord, how wonderful and extraordinary is this vision I see manifested in Your cosmic body! All of the variegated forms of organic life have been assembled here, along with the creative and destructive potentates sitting on beautiful lotus flowers. All the great philosophers and saints, as well as many benevolent wizards, are visible there. (14–15)

I cannot find out the limits of this universal feature of Yours, which appears to possess an infinity of dimensions. It seems to have no borders, no centre and no source. How grand is this vision of Your all-embracing figure, O sovereign and majestic Ruler of the cosmos! (16)

The radiant glow of Your complexion is as brilliant as the sun, and this effulgence has made it difficult for me to gain a clear vision of Your inner form, which is beyond human imagination – a sea of royal figures crowned with jewelled diadems, holding holy sceptres and wheels of power. (17)

You are the highest goal of self-realisation, and You can never be destroyed by any force. You are the infinite ground upon which the universes are constructed, and the eternal religious principles are safeguarded by You alone. It is my judgement that You are the Supreme Divine Person. (18)

There was never a time of Your beginning, nor will there be a time when You will come to Your end, or even to Your midpoint. You are of invincible stature, possessed of the force of millions of arms; the light of the sun and the moon is coming from Your eyes, the cosmic fire is pouring out of Your mouths, and Your aura is giving warmth to all creation. (19)

In this unitary figure, You permeate heaven and Earth and all directions. O Almighty Lord, an alarm is being felt throughout the whole world while I gaze upon this miraculous, yet overwhelming form of Yours. (20)

The assembly of saints is marching into You in fear and trembling. Hands folded in prayer, they invoke auspiciousness by reciting suitable verses from the Holy Scriptures. (21)

All of the godly overlords, the revered ancestors, the choirs of angels and the congregations of perfect and powerful beings are gazing upon You, awestricken. (22)

To be confronted with the reality of the scope of this mighty form of Yours, with its numberless and mighty limbs, broad and sturdy trunks and shining rows of teeth, would bring tribulation into the heart of anyone in this world, and so it has done to me. Observing the gleaming rainbow-coloured light of Your form projecting throughout outer space and seeing Your wide-open mouths and radiant, mighty eyes, my soul is overwhelmed, my heart unsteady and my mind feverish. (23–24)

To You, Who are the shelter of all the worlds, I make my plea. O Lord of Lords, show Your mercy upon me! I can no longer face this vision, which seems to have the power of the fire that annihilates the universe at the time of the final cataclysm! (25)

It appears as if the ambitious Duryodhana and his brothers, along with all the militaristic kings, are running headlong into Your gaping mouths. Our grandfather Bhishma, our teacher Drona and low-born Karna, as well as the greatest generals of our own alliance, are meeting their ends by having their heads crushed between Your deadly teeth. (26–27)

Human civilisation's greatest heroes have formed streams flowing into the vast caverns of Your mouths, just like so many mighty rivers emptying into the ocean. (28)

The people of the world are running at lightning speed to their destruction, just like moths flying to their fiery deaths. (29)

O Lord, while swallowing, You are consuming entire planets, and the radiance of Your body is filling up the entire cosmos, sending down a scorching heat. (30)

Please be kind to me and help me to understand what Your nature is. I prostrate myself before this mighty form of Yours and submit with all humility that I cannot fathom why You appear in such a devastating way.' (31)

"The Almighty Lord replied:

'I am Time, whose destructive force levels all, and My mission in coming to this sacred field is to rid the world of all the people assembled here. Even if you refuse to participate in the fighting, the soldiers of both alliances are all doomed to die. (32)

Arise, therefore, and gain glory by bringing defeat to these men who have become the world's enemies. I have already sentenced them all to death as a result of their previous actions, and I ask you now to simply carry out My will, O most expert of bowmen, as a prosperous empire will then be yours to rule and serve. (33)

There is no question of you killing Drona, Bhishma, Jayadratha, Karna, or any of the other soldiers assembled here, because they have all been slain by Me already. Therefore, you need not doubt your victory. Just stand up with resolution and courage and prepare to triumph!' " (34)

Sanjaya then related Arjuna's reaction to Dhiritarashtra:

"The terrified Arjuna folded his hands respectfully in prayer after hearing these prophetic words from the Lord, and then, with a heart filled with tribulation, he began to address Shri Krishna in the following words:

'O Lord of all the sentient beings, it is certainly most proper that Your praises are sung by loving souls throughout the universe and that all the most highly evolved amongst humanity kneel down to You in worship. Only those of atheistic temperament cover their ears and try to flee from You. (35–36)

And why should not all the universe bow down to You, Who are the greatest of all, the original father and creator of everyone and everything? You are the cause of existence and non-existence, and are the highest limit of transcendence. (37)

You are the original Supreme Divine Person, the most ancient of all living entities, and the transcendental shelter which everyone within the world is seeking. You can understand everything, and You are everything which needs to be understood. Your sacred Realm is supreme and transcendental, and by Your infinite cosmic form the whole universe is permeated. (38)

You are the controlling principle of the wind, the fire, the waters and the moon, and the original grandsire of the first progenitors of life. I could offer a thousand tributes to You and still go on to offer another and another. Please be so kind as to accept my most humble obeisances. (39)

Seeing You as the centre of everything, I salute You from every side. Your potencies are immeasurable, and all existence rests within Your mighty hands. Therefore, nothing can be seen as separate from You. (40)

Invincible You are and without limits. Please excuse, therefore, the familiarity I have shown in addressing You with friendly terms of endearment. Never understanding Your greatness, I have simply called You out of affection, saying, "O Krishna", "O Yadava", "O brother". Perhaps it was my foolish innocence, or maybe I was blinded by my love. My frivolous manners must have often offended You while we were relaxing peacefully together, sitting on the same couch and taking our meals with one another, so I humbly beg Your pardon. (41–42)

All creation can trace its paternity to You, both the living creatures and the inanimate objects. You are the inner spiritual guide of everyone and are truly worthy of the homage of all. No one can equal or excel You, and no one in all the worlds can estimate the true extent of Your glories. (43)

I offer myself at Your holy feet, praying that You will bestow Your divine grace upon me. I see clearly now that You are the Lord, the most praiseworthy and true, and I pray that You will overlook my faults out of love, just as a father may forgive the debt of a son, a brother may excuse the misdeed of his brother, or a wife may overlook the faults of her husband. (44–45)

O thousand-armed form of the universe, take away this blinding vision and please appear to me instead in Your princely form of Narayana, with four arms holding Your mighty sceptre and discus, Your auspicious conch shell and fragrant lotus.' (46)

"The Lord then spoke:

'It has been My pleasure to grant you this revelation of the form of unlimited energy by which I maintain My presence within the universe. This infinite and primal feature of Mine which I have shown you by an exercise of My inner powers has never been seen before by any mortal. (47)

Only through a special dispensation have you been able to see this mighty form, which would not have been revealed to anyone, even though they might have studied all the Holy Scriptures, carried out all sorts of pious works and performed many years of severe penances. (48)

But now let your mind be relieved of the awesome vision. Put away all tribulation and concentrate your vision once again upon My pleasing, personal features.' " (49)

Sanjaya reported:

"While speaking in such a consoling way, Lord Krishna then revealed His all-pervasive, four-armed feature, and then again was seen in His beautiful and eternal two-armed form. (50)

Seeing once more the familiar form of his friend, Arjuna then spoke:

'My dear Lord, my consciousness has become peaceful by gazing again upon this beautiful and gentle, divine form of Yours, which appears so like the human. The natural balance has again been restored to my system!' (51)

"The charming and gracious Lord responded:

'Even the denizens of the celestial paradises are always aspiring for a glimpse of this form which stands before you now, so rare it is for anyone to see. (52)

To see Me thus, in My eternal form of mystic beauty, is a reward never earned by speculative scholars. Ordinary acts of worship, generous giving in charity, long hours of abstinence and penance, great scholarship in the Scriptures – none of this can bring one the chance to see Me in My eternal form of mystery and grace. (53)

It has become possible for you to gain this vision directly and to enter into a deep understanding of the Truth of My existence only because you love Me with a heart undistracted by selfish desire. (54)

O worthy son of Pandu, all those who serve Me with loving hearts, having disassociated themselves from the tendency to exploit others, become cleansed of all impurities and come, at last, to live with Me.' " (55)

THE TWELFTH CHAPTER

Divine Communion
Through Pure Love

"Arjuna then inquired:

'There are those who say that You are beyond the range of sense perception and that Your ultimate nature is unmanifest and formless. They attempt through contemplation to understand the Supreme Truth as such. There are others who perpetually serve You with loving devotion, simply attempting to please You personally. Kindly tell me which of the two paths will lead to more perfect communion with You.' (1)

"Arjuna's Divine Teacher replied:

'I consider those who always render loving service to Me with hearts filled with deep faith and trust to be by far the best. (2)

Nonetheless, those with a less definitive idea of My real nature, who contemplate the Absolute Truth as being featureless, invincible, all-permeating, inconceivable, immobile and without inner dynamism, may come to Me in the end if they learn to achieve control over their sensual demands, gain freedom from all intellectual prejudice, and become devoted to the ideal of rendering service to all living beings. (3–4)

However, to advance towards the goal of life is neither easy nor pleasant for those whose consciousness is fixed upon My undifferentiated feature. (5)

Those who offer everything which comes from their work to Me, who are exclusively devoted to Me in love, and who make Me the object of their contemplation, find that I have very quickly arranged for their rescue from the fearsome waters of the ocean of perpetual birth and death. (6–7)

Therefore, simply absorb your consciousness in remembrance of Me and apply your intelligence in My service, and without doubt you will live with Me forever. (8)

If you find yourself unable to absorb your consciousness spontaneously and continually in Me, then you should carry out the practice of those devotional principles which will help you to increase your aspiration to reach Me. (9)

If you are unable to follow all of the principles of devotional practice, then simply try your best to serve Me, for this will bring you gradually to the platform of true perfection. (10)

If, however, you cannot come to the point of taking shelter of My Divine Service, then you should seek self-contentment by offering all of the fruits of your labours in the service of others. (11)

Those who understand the Truth are superior to those who simply practise to understand it, and those who absorb themselves deeply in contemplative trance directly perceiving the Truth are better still. Best of all, however, are those who remain ever-fixed in the ecstatic bliss of rendering active and loving service to Me. (12)

How dear to Me are My devotees! They never cherish malice towards anyone. In fact, they feel everyone to be a friend, are compassionate and kind towards all, have no tendency to exploit the environment, and never consider themselves to be the ultimate enjoyer or controller. They are equipoised in the face of both distressful and pleasant situations, forgiving of the trespasses of others and eternally satisfied by dint of engaging body, mind and soul with firm determination in My transcendental, loving service. (13–14)

My dear devotees are careful not to cause annoyance to others and are never deluded by anger, frustration and fear. (15)

Free from craving, pure at heart, ingenious and carefree, those devoted souls remain detached in the midst of all their undertakings. (16)

Filled with love for Me, they never hanker after mundane pleasure, lament or feel self-pity, and they take no thought of auspicious or inauspicious omens. (17)

My pure devotees love their enemies as much as their friends, offer all respects to others while never requiring any for themselves, and take no great thought of change of climate or of upturns and downturns of fate. They free themselves from all impure habits, are content with whatever comes to them unsought, possess a holy peace and are self-satisfied.

With hearts filled with devotion and minds fixed with determination they wander as pilgrims in the world. (18–19)

I cannot express how dear to Me are My devotees! Taking love for Me to be their all in all, illuminated by faith, they come to drink the nectar of understanding that the supreme law of life is pure love.' " (20)

THE THIRTEENTH CHAPTER

The Field of Experience and the Culture of Wisdom

"Arjuna inquired:

'Please explain the distinction between the field of experience and the experiencer who is aware of it. In addition, help me to understand the ontology of the predominated aspect of reality in its relationship to the Supreme Predominator. Finally, let me know what is wisdom and what it is that the wise seek to understand.' (1)

"The Lord, Who is all-knowing, then replied:

'My dear Kaunteya, the material body is itself the field of experience, whereas the living being who owns the body and is conscious of its activities is actually quite distinct from it. (2)

I tell you with authority that the truly wise understand this distinction between the body and the conscious soul who inhabits it, and they also know that I am sitting alongside every soul and am, therefore, also aware of what is being experienced in every field. (3)

I would like you now to listen carefully as I summarise the constituents of the field of experience and the nature of the transformations it undergoes, as well as its origins. (4)

Wise teachers throughout the ages have spoken very beautifully about the inter-relationship between matter and spirit. The verses of the Holy Vedanta, which are presented in a most reasonable and authoritative manner, are especially illuminating in this regard. (5)

Solids, liquids, gases, fire, empty space, the veil over the ego, the power of intellection, matter in its potential state before specific manifestation, the faculties of hearing, touching, seeing, tasting and smelling, the organ of speech, the legs with their power of locomotion, the dextrous hands, the computating mind, the organs of evacuation, the organs of reproduction, audible sounds, perceptible surfaces, visible forms, distinctive flavours and the various odours – these twenty-four components are the constituent elements of the field of experience. As they undergo transformations and interact with one another, specific desires and aversions develop, pleasure and pain are experienced, a constant chain of thoughts and feelings are manifested, and various convictions and beliefs develop. (6–7)

The culture of wisdom necessitates a humble state of mind, freedom from hypocritical attitudes, absence of violent and aggressive feelings, patience, forgiveness and innocence of heart. Those who hope to become wise must approach a genuine Divine Master, a wise professor who knows the truths of life. One should be clean and pure within and without and fully determined to reach perfection. The impetuous senses must be kept under control, and the heart must be devoid of the tendency to exploit others. One must be able to look beyond the veil which covers the real identity of the self, and thus become free from the selfishness which causes isolation from all others.

A realistic view of the miseries of perpetually being born and dying, becoming old and contracting disease should be developed. One should be detached from the things of the world and should see the whole universe as home and all living entities as dear relations. In this way one must escape from the provincial mentality of the narrow-minded and embrace a universal view. Understanding that both desirable and undesirable events occur in due course of time, one should learn to be equal to both. Those who hope to be counted amongst the wise should reside in a quiet place above the hustle and bustle of the worldly-minded and engage there uninterruptedly in pure devotional practices, culturing a feeling of love for Me within their hearts. Eschewing the company of those with no interest in spiritual life, those who know clearly the value of spiritual realisation should devote their time to gaining a perfect understanding of the ancient and eternal path which leads to wisdom and the vision of Absolute Truth. To adopt any other course besides the one which I have just outlined will cause one to remain within the realms of darkness and ignorance. (8–12)

I shall speak now of the eternal spirit, for it is knowledge of the spirit which constitutes the proper subject matter for study. Those who come to know that the individual spiritual personalities are all eternal, subordinate directly to Me, and transcendental to the mundane laws of cause and effect are enabled by such understanding to drink the nectar of life everlasting. (13)

The Supreme Spiritual Person is all-pervasive, with hands extended everywhere, accepting the offerings of all and awarding all benedictions, with legs extended everywhere, walking alongside each soul as well as inhabiting empty space, and with faces pointed in all directions, seeing everything and hearing every sound that is made within creation. (14)

Sensory perception originates with the Supreme Sentient Person, Who employs no mundane senses, although perceiving everything, and Who is never implicated in the affairs of the world, although being the sustainer of all that lives. This all-pervasive Supreme Person is the ultimate source of all the binding forces of material nature, and yet remains unaffected by any of them. (15)

Everyone should see the Supreme Divine Person within their own hearts as well as in the outside world, in all that lives and moves, and in all inanimate objects. Although, in one sense inconceivable and far away from everyone, the transcendental Supreme Person is, at the same time, the nearest and dearest friend of all. (16)

Although the Supreme Divine Person is by nature indivisible, infinite divisions manifest inconceivably in order that each individual being may be dealt with personally. The Supreme Person alone supplies the necessities of life to all and controls both evolution and disintegration. (17)

Whatever emanates light derives its luminescence from the Supreme Divine Person, Who is without any trace of darkness and Who, as the perfect goal of all spiritual inquiry, remains seated within the heart of every living being. (18)

I conclude here My analysis of the field of experience and its experiencer, the culture of wisdom and its proper object. It should be noted, however, that only those devoted souls who possess pure love for Me shall be able to come to a proper understanding of all this and thereby enter into intimacy with Me. (19)

Material nature has no beginning in time, and neither do the living beings. All of the specific qualities manifested within the material elements, as well as all of the transformations which matter undergoes as it changes states, arise as permutations of the essential material substance, the predominated aspect of reality. (20)

Although the changes which each body and mind go through in the course of time may be directly traced to the natural forces inherent within this essential material substance, each living being is, in fact, personally responsible for the feelings of joy and sorrow which they experience. (21)

Every person living in the world is encased within the material substance, and by associating with its various binding forces they enter in series into a wide variety of auspicious and inauspicious wombs and encounter a great range of painful and pleasurable circumstances. (22)

Within each body alongside the individual soul, the Supreme Person resides, witnessing all events, giving guidance as the inner voice of conscience, and remaining always as the ultimate enjoyer and controller of everything. This Supreme Personality is transcendental to the material substance and all its permutations. (23)

Anyone who comes to understand the transcendental position of the Supreme Divine Person and one's own position as an eternal spiritual person, as well as the nature of the essential material substance and its various qualities and transformations, will never be forced to take birth again within darkness. (24)

Some souls gain the vision of the Supreme Person by entering into contemplative trance and perceiving the transcendental Realm directly with developed spiritual vision. Others enter into a systematic analysis of all phenomena and, in this way, hope to trace out the essential nature of the universe. Some souls practise a variety of spiritual processes aimed at entering into communion with the Supreme Truth, whilst there are also others who hope to understand the Absolute by carrying out devotional activities within the world. (25)

Many persons who languish without spiritual understanding take up the sacred path of Divine Service after beginning to hear about the Supreme Person from those who are already conversant with the topics of transcendental life. Because they show an inclination to hear from authoritative sources, they also enter into everlasting life. (26)

O most worthy heir of the great King Bharata, please try to understand that the field of experience, with its twenty-four subdivisions, and the living beings, who are aware of the field due to interacting with it, produce, by their combinations, all the phenomena, both animate and inanimate, that fill up creation. (27)

Those who see clearly are able to perceive that the Supreme Divine Person loves every living being equally and remains forever alongside each individual. Such seers of the Truth know that the Supreme Person and the infinity of living beings, who are part and parcel of the Supreme, remain unchanged despite all mundane transformations, and are indestructible even though all else may be destroyed. (28)

Those who are able to see the Supreme Person everywhere, as well as in the hearts of everyone, never cause themselves grief, and very quickly arrive at the supreme goal of life by entering into their eternal Homeland, the sacred Realm of the Supreme Person. (29)

The perfect vision of such souls leads them to understand that it is material nature which is responsible for all mundane phenomena, whereas the individual spiritual persons, being non-material, are never directly affected by mundane changes and are never personally productive of them. (30)

Such souls reach the platform of perfect understanding after coming to an awareness from authoritative evidence that all diversities have their origin in a single unitary source. (31)

Aware of the eternal and free from the contamination of mundane association, the individual soul can open up the doors to the region of infinite transcendence, even while dwelling within the material body. (32)

Just as the most subtle of elements, the ether, permeates the more gross ones, although remaining unmixed with any of them, so the eternal spiritual persons pervade the material bodies but are never changed in their inherent natures by such association. (33)

My dear Arjuna, just as the shining sun pervades the entirety of creation with its brilliant rays, so the living soul pervades the body with the light of consciousness. (34)

Anyone whose eyes are illuminated with true wisdom and who understands the distinction between unconscious matter and conscious spirit is able to gain freedom from material influences and enter into the Realm of perfect transcendence.' " (35)

THE FOURTEENTH CHAPTER

The Three Binding Forces of Material Nature

"The Master of all Masters then spoke:

'I shall instruct you once more in the most sublime doctrines of ancient wisdom, through which the learned philosophers have achieved the pinnacle of perfection in their pursuit of transcendence. (1)

Protected by this perfect understanding, the wise perceive their qualitative oneness with Me and attain that region which lies beyond the perpetual cycle of creation and annihilation. (2)

All sentient beings develop from embryos within the womb of material nature, having been placed there as seeds by Me, My dear Arjuna. (3)

I am the Supreme Father Who plants the living seeds within the fertile womb of Mother Nature, allowing for the birth of all the varied forms of creatures. (4)

The eternally living spiritual persons, although unchangeable, having come to inhabit bodies composed of mundane substance, appear to be transformed by the modulations of the three binding forces of that substance – the harmonising force of goodness, the energising force of passion, and the darkening force which exercises an inertial effect. (5)

Those persons who are more influenced by goodness become bound by attachment to the feelings of happiness which this harmonising force produces. By comparison to the others, this mode may be seen as free from taint, O pure hearted Arjuna. (6)

You should understand that the principle of mundane attraction, born of the energising mode of nature, gives rise to passionate endeavour which, in turn, leads one to be bound by attachment to the fruits gained by one's efforts. (7)

All embodied persons are subject to the inebriating effect of contact with the darkening force, and as a result of such connection, misunderstanding, inertia and excessive sleep, which cover one in nescience, arise. (8)

Actions performed with good motives are productive of real happiness, whereas actions based on selfish ambition bind one to the fruits. Under the spell of darkness, the natural wisdom of the soul becomes clouded over and various forms of insanity are manifested. (9)

Every person is influenced by different mixtures of purity, passion and darkness. For some time, purity remains in ascendancy over passion and darkness; then again, passion will rise and become prevalent and, in due course, darkness will overshadow both purity and passion. (10)

When the sensory gates are opened and filled with light and mental insight has become sharp and clear, the innate goodness of the living soul may be sensed. (11)

As the influence of passion increases, there arises a tendency towards gluttony, a voracious appetite to enjoy the things of the world, and self-centred ambition becomes the motivation for all action. (12)

O favourite child of the family of Kuru, as darkness ascends, consciousness dwindles, inertia takes hold, symptoms of neurosis are seen, and a person becomes increasingly bewildered by illusion. (13)

Those persons who begin the journey which commences upon the leaving of their bodies after having become established in pure goodness gain entrance to those immaculate regions inhabited by the seers of the Truth. (14)

Those who leave their bodies while under the dominance of passion take rebirth in the human civilisation amongst the fruitive workers, whereas those who depart while under a predominant influence of darkness enter thereafter the wombs of the most ignorant of creatures. (15)

By carrying out good works in the spirit of service to others, the soul becomes purified of all contaminations, whereas by acting under the impulse of selfish desires, only suffering results. To act under the spell of darkness binds one to a life of ignorance. (16)

Wisdom is born through the agency of the harmonising force; insatiable desire arises from the impassioning force; and insanity, confusion and ignorance develop by the effect of the darkening force. (17)

Those affected by the harmonising force of goodness evolve upwards and taste paradise; those under influence of the impassioning force remain struggling within the human society; whilst those heavily affected by the darkening force, on account of the abominable nature of their activities, may find their consciousness constricted within the bodies of animals. (18)

Those who are able to see clearly come to understand the workings of these forces, and they see all mundane causes and effects as functions of their interactions. Through culture of such clear vision they become transcendental to all mundane influences and enter their eternal Homeland, the sacred Realm of the Supreme Divine Person. (19)

If the effects of these three forces can be overcome, it is possible for a person to gain complete freedom from all of the miseries of material existence and to relish the ambrosia of life everlasting, even while within the body.' (20)

"Arjuna then inquired:

'O my dearmost Master, how may I come to ascertain which souls have actually overcome the influence of all the forces of mundane nature? What sort of character will they display, and how is it that they become established in such transcendence?' (21)

"The kind and gentle Lord then replied:

'Those who are fixed in transcendence sit as impartial observers while the various effects of the different mundane forces manifest themselves. They show neither attachment nor aversion to any of the effects, never longing for one or dreading another, accepting pleasure and pain with equal indifference, seeing gold to have no greater intrinsic value than ordinary stone, and looking with equal favour upon that which is near and dear and that which is repulsive. They do not hanker for flattery and praise, take no offence when criticised and defamed, love both allies and adversaries, and never endeavour for mundane success. (22–25)

Those who follow the sacred path of unalloyed Divine Service, communing with Me in transcendental love, are automatically freed from all mundane effects and are enabled to perceive the Realm of pure divine consciousness, that everlasting zone of nectar, which is the domain of Supreme Truth and infinite joy and which has its foundations in Me.'" (26–27)

THE FIFTEENTH CHAPTER

The Supermost
of All Personalities

"The sanctuary of supreme joy, Lord Krishna, then said:

'By way of analogy, we may contemplate upon material creation as a great banyan tree whose extensive root system spreads upward to gain sustenance from the primal energies of the Supreme Person. Its branches, the different species of life, in turn grow downwards and then extend in all directions. The three binding forces of material nature are like nutrients drawn up through the roots to bring about the growth of the various types of senses and sense objects, which are represented by the twigs and stems. Conditioned actions within human civilisation form the subsidiary roots, which give further strength to the tree, and the verses of scripture, which prescribe the means to gradually progress within the realms of matter, are the tree's leaves. (1–2)

Caught up in the branches of this vast tree, the soul is unable to perceive the true form of the tree, its real foundation, its origin or its full extent. One must therefore strive to become disconnected from this tree of mundane energy by cutting at its roots with the sharp sword of genuine renunciation. (3)

Thereafter, one should seek entrance into the Supreme Spiritual Abode, the place of everlasting life and love. Therein, one must practise the ways of loving and surrendered service in the company of the Supreme Divine Person, the ancient source of all emanations. (4)

Life everlasting in the eternal Homeland, the sacred Realm of the Supreme Person, is readily available to those unconfused souls whose consciousness is beyond desiring for false prestige, unencumbered by defective conceptions, fully aware of the eternality of the spirit, disinterested in mundane enjoyments, and equal in pleasure and pain. (5)

My Supreme Abode is self-luminous, and therefore has no need for the light of suns, moons or fires. Those who become fully conscious of it never again lose that awareness. (6)

All of the eternal, individual living beings are expanded portions of My own Self. However, conditioned by connection with material nature, they remain as if shackled by the mind and senses. (7)

Just as fragrance leaves a flower and is carried far away by the breeze, so the living being leaving one body carries the subtle impressions of the last life into the next one. (8)

Applying consciousness to a particular grouping of senses, the soul enjoys the sounds heard through the ears, the sights seen by the eyes, the objects encountered by the tactile sense, the flavours perceived by the tongue, the fragrances entering the nose, and the stream of thought flowing through the mind. (9)

The unenlightened cannot understand how the conscious soul, being distinct from the body, sometimes dwells within the body and enjoys the world and sometimes departs from it. Neither can they understand how the changing forces of material nature affect the conditions which the soul encounters in this world. Only those fortunate souls whose vision is illuminated with perfect understanding are able to see this all clearly. (10)

Those whose aspiration for Divine Communion with Me has inspired them to become established in self-realisation become directly aware of the truth concerning these matters, whereas those whose consciousness is immature remain ignorant of this and absorbed in more rudimentary conceptions. (11)

The brilliance of the sun's effulgence by which the whole creation is illumined, the soothing light of the moon which bathes the earth at night, and the useful glow of fire – all of these should be understood as emanating from Me. (12)

Being present within the earth, I maintain her in her orbit and give sustenance to all the forms of life which dwell upon her. I instill healing potency into all medicinal plants and pleasing flavour into all vegetables by My activation of the lunar cycle, and I release the transcendental and mellow flavours of divine ecstasy by becoming the juice of Soma. (13)

I am the active agent who energises the process of digestion in the bodies of all living creatures; I am the breath of life, the incoming air which nourishes the blood and allows for the metabolic process to go on and the outgoing air which is recycled into the environment. (14)

I am installed as the Deity within the sanctum sanctorum of everyone's heart; the ability to remember comes from Me; true wisdom and perfect understanding come from Me, as does the very power of rational thinking. The purpose of all the Holy Scriptures is to bring souls into remembrance of Me. I am, in fact, the true author of all the sacred writings, and I perfectly understand the true import and conclusion of all authoritative scriptural texts. (15)

Within the world we may observe two types of persons – the mortal and the immortal. Although all persons are subjected to death, those who have become united with Me in Divine Communion can never, in actual fact, be defeated by death, because they are linked beyond all questions of mortality and immortality with the infinite Sovereign of the galaxies, Who lives on and remains the supermost of all personalities. (16–17)

Throughout the many lands of the world and throughout the many pages of the Holy Scriptures, I am glorified as that Supermost Divinity, the transcendent Supreme Person, Who lies beyond the destructible world and Who is the very source of the multitudes of imperishable souls. (18)

Those fortunate souls who develop the absolute conviction that I am personally the Supreme Lord are able thereby to understand everything clearly and therefore absorb themselves in serving Me with loving devotion, My dear Arjuna. (19)

O My pure-hearted friend, give full credence to these words of Mine, which contain the clues whereby the most confidential of all revelations may be gained. Anyone who applies the power of intellect sincerely to this subject matter will come to possess infinite wisdom and experience total satisfaction.' " (20)

THE SIXTEENTH CHAPTER

Divine Communion Through Discrimination Between Good and Evil

"The Supreme Lord said:

'Certain qualities come to ornament the personalities of those who are inclined to the divine life. They become truly fearless, absolutely pure at heart and filled with wisdom. Always absorbed in communion with Me, they give generously in service to others, practise self-discipline and joyfully participate in acts of divine worship, singing My Holy Names and dancing in ecstasy. By contemplation of the Holy Scriptures, they come to understand the deepest meanings of a life of Divine Service and show preference for a simple life, in tune with the natural flow. They transcend all aggressive feelings and show kindness to all. Ever-attached to truth and always pleasant in their speaking, they never become inflamed with anger. Turning their back on materialistic pursuits, they achieve perfect tranquillity. They never like to see the defects of others, preferring to show their love and mercy towards all. Never greedy for mundane achievement, they are mild-mannered, gentle, humble and kind. They work with resolute purpose, are filled with vitality and strength, never take offence at anything and are always ready to forgive the failings of others. Filled with courage on account of their deep faith, they remain always free of mundane taint and pray for the well-being of all. Although they are the most honourable of all souls, they never desire praise and are never pompous. So wonderful are the qualities of My devotees! (1–3)

On the other hand, My dear child of Pritha, those of atheistic temperament are generally hypocrites, filled with pride and arrogance and anxious to see themselves as the centre of the universe. They are easily moved to anger, deal very roughly with others and are dull-witted, never able to penetrate into the real meaning of life. (4)

O orphaned son of the great King Pandu, fear not! You possessed the inclination towards divine life even at the time of your birth. Supreme redemption comes quickly to those whose devotional qualities are manifest, but continued confinement within the limits of matter is the fate of those who show no love for others. (5)

Two types of persons are to be found in this world: the saintly hearted and the evil-minded. I have described already in some detail the qualities of the devoted and spiritually minded souls, but I shall now discuss the nature of those with flawed understanding, who cannot come to share in the reservoir of divine qualities. (6)

The evil-minded are blind to truth, their character is obnoxious and their habits unclean. They are unable to distinguish properly between action that will be truly beneficial and action that will cause distress. (7)

They conclude that life is without real meaning and that the cosmos has no absolute foundation. As for consciousness, they presume that it is merely a biological function. (8)

The consciousness of such persons remains crippled by such misconceptions and therefore deprived of its true glory. Because their ethical conceptions are unevolved, they carry out their misguided schemes with a view towards exploiting the environment and other souls for personal gain. At last, they will conceive and construct devices that are capable of destroying the whole world. (9)

They approach their unclean works with determination and find refuge in the temporary satisfaction of their passionate drives. Puffed up with self-importance and overbearing in their mannerisms, they deceive even their very selves and are unable to distinguish reality from mirage. (10)

They think that the satisfaction of their selfish desires is the ultimate purpose of life and are, therefore, always uneasy and beset with cares. Only death comes at last to relieve their anxieties. (11)

Filled with false hopes and bound within a framework built of their numberless desires, they become frustrated and easily rise to anger. Requiring wealth to satisfy their sensual appetites, they are never constrained by conscience from adopting even unfair means which might bring harm to others. (12)

Evil-minded persons calculate in their darkness, thinking: "I have already gained much by my cleverness, and I am determined to acquire much more in days to come. My assets will no doubt increase manifold as time goes on. I have already succeeded in eliminating several of my opponents and competitors, and will make sure to get rid of the rest of them before long. I am the only real God because by my own efforts everything can be put under control. In fact, everything is simply meant for my pleasure because I am the most perfect of all and the most potent as well. So happy I am, enjoying my opulence in the midst of my high-class relatives and friends! I shall perpetuate this pleasure by gaining fame as a philanthropist and a man of piety and, in this way, I shall be triumphant". (13–15)

With their consciousness always overburdened by such involved calculations, they find themselves imprisoned within the web of their own misconceptions and thus, although their desire for enjoyment is very strong, they end up in a hellish condition, tortured by their own impurities. (16)

Fully convinced of their own superiority, shameless in their exploitation of others, concerned only with acquiring wealth and gaining name and fame, they participate in community affairs or take part in religious activities only to make a show of piety. They never consider scriptural injunctions to be authoritative. (17)

Always misidentifying themselves with the body and mind, dependent on their own limited strength, proud of their mundane achievements, driven by numberless desires and easily displeased and angered, those whose hearts are contaminated with malice towards others come to despise the Supreme Person Who dwells within the hearts of all, and they fill their mouths with blasphemies and unkind words. (18)

Being the least evolved of all the human race, such envious and cruel persons wander continuously from one inauspicious womb to another. In this way, I keep them circling within the wheel of perpetual birth and death. (19)

Birth after birth passes for such ungodly souls and, never seeking to reach Me, they spiral downwards condemned to enter one place of darkness after another. (20)

There are three doors which open up to hellish existence. These are marked: "Craving for Sense Pleasure", "Angry Feelings Towards Others" and "Avarice and Gluttony". Therefore, one should keep these three doors firmly closed and bolted. (21)

O noble son of the pious Queen Kunti, any person who transcends these paths to darkness comes to display transparently the true and divine character of the soul and enters, at last, into the sacred Homeland, the eternal Realm of the Supreme Divine Person. (22)

However, those who place no faith in the Holy Scriptures, but do whatever they please to satisfy their selfish desires, never reach the platform of perfection and never come to taste the joy of everlasting life in My Supreme Abode. (23)

Therefore, one must contemplate deeply upon the Holy Scriptures and understand from authoritative evidence found therein what kind of action will lead to degradation and what kind will elevate one to the perfectional stage of life.' " (24)

THE SEVENTEENTH CHAPTER

Varieties of Faiths, Foods, and Sacrifices

"Arjuna then placed another query:

'My dear Lord, please explain the effects of the three binding forces of mundane nature upon the faith of those persons who possess no great regard for the advices of the Holy Scriptures.' (1)

"The Supreme Person, Who possesses all forms of wealth, beauty, wisdom, prestige, potency and loving compassion in abundance, then replied:

'Please listen carefully as I explain how persons who are embodied within a consciousness of the mundane develop a variety of faith and belief patterns, differing from one another on account of the varying degrees by which each is affected by the purifying, impassioning and darkening forces of mundane nature. (2)

The substance of all true theistic faith is pure goodness, and it is such faith that lies potentially at the heart of every person. Yet, according to the varied effects of the mundane energies, particular modifications occur, and different persons develop different faiths and belief structures, come to identify themselves as followers of different sects, and adhere to different world views. (3)

Those persons who are more heavily influenced by the harmonising and purifying force of nature devote themselves to the worship of various divinities; those who are under heavy influence of the energising and impassioning force offer homage to wealthy and powerful materialists, worshipping a variety of heroes; and those who are under the spell of darkness worship ghosts or satanic beings. (4)

There is a class of persons who torment their minds and bodies by practising too severe an asceticism. They do this under the impulse of false pride, being unable to understand their true spiritual identity. In fact, it is the subtle force of their attachment to sense-pleasures that moves them to such severity. (5)

You should understand that those who mistreat their bodies with the hope of spiritual attainment thereby mistreat Me, the Supreme Person Who dwells within the body, and therefore their behaviour is, in fact, most ungodly. (6)

Listen further as I explain how persons adopt different diets and become attracted to different sorts of foods under the varying influences of the three mundane forces. Their tendency to carry out diverse religious liturgies, to perform various penances and to give of themselves in charitable work is also affected by the ever-changing influences of modulating nature. (7)

As far as diet is concerned, there are certain foods which promote longevity, purify the blood, increase bodily strength, help to prevent disease, add to happiness and bring about ever-greater satisfaction. Such foods are filled with flavour, freshness and natural vitality and will prove pleasing even to the heart. Persons who are purified and in harmony with nature's force of goodness naturally choose such delightful foods when making up their diets. (8)

A taste for very bitter, very sour or overly hot and spicy foods develops by the influence of the impassioning mode of nature. Passion also causes persons to eat foods which are unhealthy and disease producing. (9)

It is under the spell of darkness that people become attracted to things with a putrid taste and smell, to decomposing meats and other untouchable foods. (10)

As far as attendance at the performance of divine liturgies is concerned, those who participate without any ulterior purpose and without any desire for mundane reward may be understood to be under the shelter of the purifying and harmonising mode of nature. (11)

Those who attend religious services with a view towards obtaining some mundane benediction or with a desire to secure social position and prestige do so under the impulse of the impassioning force, O most worthy heir of the dynasty descending from King Bharata. (12)

Those religious services which are performed without any reference to Holy Scripture, without the consecration and distribution of divine food, without the proper glorification of the Holy Names of the Supreme Divinity, without sacrifice of any of one's worldly possessions and without genuine faith take place as a result of the influence of the mode of darkness. (13)

Certain moral strictures are incumbent upon embodied souls. They should be active in service to the Supreme Person, to saintly persons, to their spiritual teachers and to elders. They must keep themselves clean and pure, within and without. They should be straightforward and honest in their dealing, should have sexual relations only within the sanctuary of marriage vows and should never do any sort of violence to others. (14)

Furthermore, certain strictures apply to the use of the organ of speech. One should speak in a pleasing way, never causing offence to others and exchanging endearing words with others in love. The names of the Supreme Person and the words of the Holy Scriptures should be often repeated as well. (15)

A certain discipline should be adopted in regard to the mind also. One should allow it to become satisfied by contemplation of lofty topics and never allow it to be duplicitous towards others. One should culture an inner earnestness appropriate to the serious nature of life. Meditating always on Divine Truth, one should bring calmness and serenity to the mind by thinking only of that which is pure and self-enriching. (16)

The purifying and harmonising mode of goodness influences faithful persons to rise to the transcendental position, enlivens them to follow the appropriate moral codes, helps them to perfect their speech, and enables them to bring perfect equilibrium to the mind. (17)

Those who follow religious strictures with a view towards enhancing personal prestige and gaining the adoration of others do so under the influence of passion. Such observances have no steady basis and, therefore, will not endure. (18)

Animalistic persons who torture their own bodies and minds through self-abuse or undergo penances with a view to harm others through occult means do so under the spell of darkness. (19)

The purifying and harmonising influence of goodness leads one to offer gifts in charity to truly worthy persons and for good causes, duly considering time, place and circumstances, and never expecting any reward or recognition. (20)

Those whose charitable work springs from an ulterior motive, such as desire for name, fame or control, and who give only out of obligation, although resenting having to do so, may be seen to be influenced by the impassioning mode of nature. (21)

Acts of charity given to unworthy recipients who will use the gifts for unwholesome purposes – things given at inappropriate times or in the wrong place and offerings made with an attitude of contempt for the recipient – are all influenced by the effects of the mode of darkness, by which the soul is kept in ignorance. (22)

Since ancient days, the sacred syllables AUM, TAT and SAT have been used by the great professors of spiritual truth in the course of their performance of the divine liturgies prescribed in the Holy Scriptures. The Supreme Spirit has always borne such a triune designation. (23)

Therefore, at the onset of every religious ceremony, before every offering of charity and at the commencement of a period of penance, those learned spiritualists who understand the codes of scripture correctly first recite the holy syllable AUM, which summarises the Absolute Truth. (24)

Understanding the syllable TAT to indicate the all-pervasiveness of the Supreme Truth, those who are on the path to supreme salvation utter this sound in the course of their selfless performance of the divine liturgies and while carrying out their vows of penance. Their giving of gifts and all of their other activities are animated by this consciousness of the inter-relatedness of all existence and absolute proprietorship of the Supreme Divine Person. (25)

My dear child of Pritha, the eternal divine substance which remains always transcendental to all mundane fluctuations is referred to by the sacred sound SAT, as are all those saintly persons who seek for the good, the true and the beautiful. Therefore, one should recite this holy and auspicious sound and contemplate the supreme objective. (26)

In the performance of all divine ceremonies, in the course of all penances and austerities, and in all voluntary and charitable works, one must contemplate the eternality of the spiritual substance and invoke the Supreme Truth. (27)

Persons who are without faith in the Supreme Divine Person and the sacred quality of life may offer gifts in charity or perform some acts of sacrifice, but such works will bring about no substantial benefit, either in this life or the hereafter, and are of no real value in absolute terms because they are without any eternal significance.' " (28)

THE EIGHTEENTH CHAPTER

Enlightenment Through Self-Surrender

"Arjuna then said:

'O my Lord! You vanquish the doubts of Your pure devotees, and in Your mighty hands the whole world is resting. You are the unlimited reservoir of transcendental feelings, from which all sentient beings derive their capacities to exist, to interact with the environment, and to exchange love. I beg, therefore, that You will enlighten me about the nature of genuine detachment from matter and about the characteristics of the real renunciate.' (1)

"The Blessed Lord replied:

'Learned philosophers who have actually realised the truths of life define genuine detachment as the complete freedom from the tendency to act on the basis of self-centred, exploitative motivations. The sages know that enthusiastic service in the spirit of dedication to the complete whole is the symptom of those who are actually renunciates. (2)

Although there is a certain school of thought that declares all action to be ultimately harmful and perfection to be attainable only through absolute retirement from work, the truly learned argue that engagement in the performance of divine liturgies, offering of services for the benefit of others, and the regular execution of spiritual practices should, in fact, at no time be given up. (3)

O crest jewel of your family, most valiant of the human race, please listen carefully as I explain authoritatively the three different levels of detachment from material affairs. (4)

Even the wisest and most exalted of persons may gain further self-enrichment by devotedly participating in those rites of divine worship in which the Supreme Divine Person is invoked and glorified. Furthermore, every soul is obligated by the higher law of love to actively try to help those in need, and should be ready to work in a true spirit of self-sacrifice. (5)

It is my conclusion that action without any trace of selfish motivation, fully animated by loving devotion, is the most praiseworthy course to adopt. (6)

Each person has a purpose in life to fulfil, and service is required from everyone. Illusion may influence a soul to abandon that service, but such neglect is due to the impulses born of darkness and is a symptom of ignorance. (7)

If, under the heavy influence of the impassioning mode of nature, one abandons the ideal of service, thinking an active life to be the source of affliction and grief, such so-called renunciation will never bring the sweet taste brought about by true detachment. (8)

In My considered opinion, when genuine detachment arises in the heart by the influence of the purifying and harmonising mode of nature, a person will carry out with joy whatever action may be required and will never act from selfish motive, being moved instead by a consciousness of the underlying unity of all existence. (9)

Enlightened intelligence and freedom from all doubts are bestowed on the truly pure at heart, who give up all self-centred conceptions of action, showing readiness to do even that which seems unpleasant, if it be their duty, and showing willingness to give up that which seems pleasing, if it be contrary to duty. (10)

Inasmuch as it is never possible to totally avoid action as long as one remains within this world, genuine detachment is not characterised by inaction, but by the willingness to offer selfless service. (11)

Fruitive workers face three prospects at the time of death. Those whose actions are predominantly pious may look forward to higher birth; those whose actions are greatly impious may slip down to a birth in some hellish condition; and those whose lives are mediocre will find continued opportunity for more of the same. However, those detached souls whose pure hearts enliven them to selfless action remain free from all necessity for rebirth. (12)

My wise and powerful friend, the Holy Scriptures explain that whatever action takes place may be analysed in terms of five different factors which necessarily contribute to its being undertaken and completed. (13)

The first factor is the physical field in which the action is being carried out, the particular type of body and the nature of the environment in which the body is to act. Secondly, the individual nature of the person carrying out the action needs to be considered. In the third place, the specific technology to be employed and the various implements to be utilised are a determining factor. The fourth point to analyse is the exact nature of that which is to be accomplished. Finally, however, the most fundamental of all of the factors involved in any action is the Will of the Supreme Person, Which is the ultimate determinant of everything. (14)

Whatever action a person may carry out physically, verbally or mentally, successfully or unsuccessfully, may be analysed in terms of these five contributing factors. (15)

Only those with unevolved intelligence are so foolish as to think themselves to be the exclusive factor determining the execution and outcome of their actions. (16)

Those who act without this false sense of overlordship, never allowing their pure power of intellection to be influenced by mundane duality, are never entangled in the chain of action and reaction. Whatever they must do, impelled by higher duty, no blame will ever be incurred by them. (17)

The inspiration to act arises when the soul is awake and aware, conscious of some particular purpose that needs to be achieved, and acquainted with the means by which that goal may be reached. When the inspiration to act is there, then the individual involved, the particular set of senses and mind being employed, and the specific work that is to be accomplished constitute the factors involved in carrying out the action. (18)

The modulation of mundane nature produces three principal modes of understanding, three different categories of activities and three different attitudes in the hearts of those that are working. Please continue to hear attentively as I explain them. (19)

In those whose hearts have been purified by the harmonising effect of goodness, an understanding of the underlying unity of all life arises, a vision of oneness in diversity. (20)

Those whose understanding is affected by the influence of the impassioning force imagine every person to be isolated and unconnected with all others. They come to the conclusion that the differentiation of external forms implies some basic inequality between beings. (21)

Those who are in ignorance, under the influence of darkness, see everything only in relationship to themselves. They are never able to ascertain what is the real shape of things and cannot properly associate causes with their effects. The understanding of such persons is formulated without any reference to higher truths and is, therefore, most deficient. (22)

The harmonising and purifying force of goodness inspires those who are genuinely attached to a pattern of activity that is in accordance with scriptural codes, without selfish motivations and free from favouritism and prejudice. (23)

To those whose hearts are affected by passion, all activity seems very laborious. Suffering on account of misidentifying themselves with their bodies and minds, they act only for selfish gratification. (24)

When activity is undertaken without any thought of future consequences, without regard for the feelings of others and without proper deliberation as to practicality, it is a symptom of the influence of darkness. (25)

Those whose efforts are illuminated by the purifying and harmonising effect of goodness show themselves to be liberated from all mundane attractions, freed from the tendency to exploit others, enthusiastic in the execution of that which is good and true, and unconcerned with favourable and unfavourable circumstances. (26)

The efforts of those impassioned by the energising force of nature are characterised by an intense attachment to enjoying the fruits of their own labours, an insatiable desire for food and wealth, a tendency towards violence and harshness, a host of impure habits, and an unstable emotional life. (27)

Those workers who are under the influence of darkness never take account of the ordinances contained in the Holy Scriptures. They are stubborn and intractable in their dealings and are always willing to mislead others. They often speak unkindly of their neighbours, are averse to hard work, are unsociable and ill-humoured, and have a tendency to put things off indefinitely. (28)

My dear Arjuna, now please hear from Me as I describe the various effects of modulating nature on intelligence and on the will to act. (29)

When the intellect is able to discern properly between appropriate and inappropriate modes of action, when it understands the causes of fear and is thereby able to attain fearlessness, when it knows the roots of bondage and the path to liberation – only then can it be said to be illuminated by the purifying and harmonising effect of goodness. (30)

When the intellect remains flawed by the influence of the impassioning force of nature, action which is in accordance with Divine Law cannot be distinguished from criminal behaviour, and that which is good and beneficial cannot be distinguished from that which is not. (31)

Those whose intellect is under the spell of darkness actually consider goodness to be evil and evil to be goodness. Ignorance clouds their vision and, therefore, they stumble blindly in the wrong direction. (32)

My dear child of Pritha, those who have been influenced by the purifying and harmonising effect of goodness possess a will to act that is consistent and sustainable. Being resolute in their determination, they are able to supervise properly all of the affairs of life and all the activities of mind and senses. Absorbing themselves continuously in Divine Communion with Me by serving Me with loving devotion, they develop an inner resolve which can never be worn down by any external factor. (33)

The will to act of those whose hearts have been influenced by the impassioning mode of nature becomes firm, but only in pursuit of the attainment of the limited goals of mundane religiosity, economic development and sensual gratification. (34)

The will to act of those who are under the spell of darkness remains weakened by excessive sleep, paranoia, grief, loss of heart and general bewilderment. (35)

The happiness experienced by souls in this world falls into three different classes, but only those who seek joy through spiritual practice are enabled to come to the end of all suffering. (36)

Although at the onset of one's spiritual life one may feel as if poisoned by the determined effort to transcend the mundane that is required of the aspirant, in the course of time that poison becomes transformed into nectar. The purifying and harmonising effect of goodness brings one real joy and enables one, at last, to taste the mercy of complete self-realisation. (37)

On the other hand, the feelings of happiness that arise when the senses come into connection with their objects bear a taste of nectar in the beginning, but later on the taste becomes like poison. Such is the inferior quality of that happiness which is enjoyed while under the jurisdiction of passion. (38)

Those unfortunate souls who are under the spell of darkness try to derive happiness in ways that are, in fact, quite horrible even from the start. They take shelter in unconsciousness, idle loafing and madness. (39)

Nowhere within the domain of matter, whether on this earth or on the planets of outer space where the *devas* reside, does anything exist which is free from the modulating influences of the three primary qualities of mundane natural forces. (40)

Priests and intellectuals, warriors and administrators, merchants and farmers, artisans and labourers – all are distinguished from one another on account of the varied influences of the binding forces of material nature. (41)

Priests and teachers should be peaceful and self-controlled. They must observe the moral strictures regulating body, mind and words. Their habits and hearts should be pure, and they should be able to endure long and much. Being noncovetous, they should be upright, sincere and truthful. As a matter of course, they must be wise, learned and thoroughly pious. (42)

Warriors and administrators should be noble and heroic. They must have the authority and the potency to carry out their responsibilities, should face their work with firm resolve, and employ all of their creative intelligence. In a battle or in a crisis, they must be valiant and level-headed and must never flee from the field in fear. They should be very generous in their dealings with the citizens and should display natural leadership qualities. (43)

Farmers and merchants must tend diligently and honestly to the production of food and other necessary items, the protection of the animals, especially cows, all matters of trade and commerce, and the system of banking. Artisans and labourers should carry out their work skilfully, honestly, and with a spirit of service to others. (44)

All persons can achieve perfection by doing that work which comes naturally to them as well as they can. Listen as I explain further. (45)

The Supreme Absolute Truth is the source of all emanations, and those fortunate human beings who offer their lives in service to that Truth can achieve perfection simply by doing that which comes naturally. (46)

It is preferable to carry out that service which is ordained for one by nature, even if one is unable to do it perfectly, than to attempt to perform the function of another, though it may seem more attractive. If one sincerely attempts to carry out God-given responsibilities, no blame will ever result. (47)

No work is without its difficulties, my dear Kaunteya. Nonetheless, one should never abandon a noble venture simply because some trouble arises, just as one does not put out a fire simply because it also produces some smoke. (48)

When the power of intellection becomes non-aligned with the forces of mundane attraction and repulsion, when one gains mastery of the self and no longer maintains any mundane ambition, when one becomes perfect in transcendental activity dedicating every thought, word and action to the loving service of the Supreme Person – at that time, one may be considered a true renunciate. (49)

I shall now present a summary study of the means by which the realisation of one's relationship with the Supreme Divine Person may be actualised. This is the mature stage of transcendental knowledge, and should be understood as such. (50)

One's intelligence must become fully cleansed by an infusion of Divine Grace, and one must seek with firm resolution to adapt all activity to the higher needs of the soul. One should attempt to hear only transcendental sound vibrations and should dedicate all of the actions of the senses to the service of the Supreme Truth, putting aside all provincial calculations and adopting a universal standpoint. One should live as a hermit or in the company of pure devotees, moderating one's consumption of food and eating only food that is sanctified first by offering to the Supreme Person. One should also be careful to control the organ of speech by always singing the glories of the Supreme and by speaking only those things which are pertinent to circumstances and have some substance. The activities of mind and senses should be overseen carefully and maturely. One should constantly remain absorbed in contemplation of the transcendence and become fixed in Divine Communion with Me. Ever-free from attachment to the mundane and temporary, one should seek the shelter of the spiritual and eternal. Freeing oneself from the tendency to exploit others, one should cultivate spiritual strength and become cleansed of false prestige, selfish desires and feelings of anger and displeasure. One should accept whatever is favourable to the execution of Divine Service and give up whatever is unfavourable. Never thinking oneself to be the true owner of anything, one should become perfectly peaceful and in harmony with all creation, and in this way one will at last become firmly established on the plane of fully realised spiritual under-standing. (51–53)

Having realised one's identity in relationship to the Supreme Truth, one naturally becomes fully self-satisfied and blissful. Never grieving over anything, never hankering for anything, one begins to see all living beings with love, and in this way one gradually achieves the platform of unalloyed pure devot-ional love for Me. (54)

The Absolute Reality can be perceived directly by a heart that has been transformed and melted by the ecstasy of unalloyed devotional love. After such transformation occurs, the Supreme Truth – the Supreme Divine Person – may be seen face to face, and one may enter into the divine and everlasting spiritual Realm. (55)

I shall forever personally guarantee protection and full security to My pure devotees, showering them lavishly with My mercy and blessings. Eternally, they will have a place in My infinite and indescribably blissful Home. (56)

Carry out all of your activities while fully absorbing your consciousness in remembrance of Me. Dedicate all of your actions to My service and feel yourself fully sheltered by My mercy. Absorbing your intelligence in deep communion with Me, you should execute pure devotional activities throughout the twenty-four hours of the day. (57)

If you simply absorb your consciousness in remembering Me, then I shall personally see that the purifying rays of My mercy will cleanse your heart of any impediment which might come to hinder you along your way. On the other hand, if you are unable to see beyond the veil covering your real identity, you will be unable to understand the divine nature of these words of Mine and be lost again in the wilderness of the mundane existence. (58)

If you surrender to the direction of your mind, which has become mystified by misconceptions regarding your own nature and the nature of the world, and if you thereby refuse to carry out your service, it will be a misuse of your free will. The dictates of your own nature will, in due course, override your decision, and you will be forced to fulfil your destiny by joining with the fight. (59)

Although, for the moment, you have succeeded in deceiving yourself and are, therefore, disinclined towards co-operating with My plans for redeeming the world, the instincts born of your own nature will, in time, propel you to the very foreground of the struggle. (60)

Within each person's heart of hearts, the Supreme Master resides. The soul, which is spontaneous and spiritual, is placed within a body which is mechanical and mundane. Transmigrating from body to body, individual eternal spiritual persons are always accompanied by the Supreme Person, Who is the ultimate overseer of everything. Yet, as if by influence of a magic spell, they remain unaware of how all this is working. (61)

Learn to follow the sacred ways of divine surrender and take shelter of the Supreme Truth with your whole heart. Mercy will then rain down upon you, and you will feel peace and well-being permeating your consciousness. At last you will enter into the sacred Realm of the Supreme Person, the everlasting Abode of absolute joy. (62)

Now the choice is yours. I have disclosed to you the most confidential aspects of the secret path of divine wisdom. Contemplate the matter deeply and come to your own conclusions. You are free to act in whatever way your conscience ultimately guides you. (63)

Out of love for you, I shall once again summarise the innermost secrets of life. Listen carefully, for the supreme transcendence may be accessed through My words. (64)

Remain ever conscious of Me and offer your heart to Me in love. Engage always in My Divine Service, remaining ever-faithful to Me. Because I love you very dearly, I make this vow to you, "You will live with Me always, and through exchange of love we will be one forever!" (65)

Laying aside all other conceptions of religious laws and duties, take up the ways of loving surrender to Me. No blame will touch you if you carry out your service in the spirit of devotional love, because I shall always stand beside you and give you My personal protection. (66)

This teaching will remain a secret to those who feel no contrition in their hearts for their misdeeds and no love in their hearts for Me. It will also remain hidden to all those who never take the time or interest to hear it and to understand the inner meanings. Finally, the doors to transcendental knowledge will remain closed to those who take pleasure in the misfortune of others and to those who are envious of My supreme position. (67)

The compassionate persons who take up the service of ministering this most sublime and secret message of Mine to the loving and faithful souls of the world perform thereby the greatest welfare work of all. By helping other persons to come closer to Me, they please Me greatly, and before long they come to live with Me. Of this there is no doubt. (68)

Throughout the whole of humanity, no one can be found who is more dear to Me than those who sincerely witness on

My behalf. Those who teach the sacred way of transcendental love by their own sincere example will always maintain the central position in My heart. (69)

The contemplation of this holy dialogue of ours is itself an exalted act of divine worship. It is my firm conviction that those who make an offering of their intelligence by trying to understand My instructions will come thereby to possess perfect wisdom. (70)

Those who listen carefully to these words with hearts filled with faith and devoid of envy are certain to gain supreme salvation. They will live in that all-auspicious plane of existence where all of the saints reside. (71)

O most fortunate of souls, dear child of Pritha, have you listened to all these words of Mine with single-pointed attention? Has the fog which darkened your heart lifted and the bewilderment which clouded your mind and will been swept away?' (72)

"Arjuna then responded as follows:

'My dear Lord, You are beyond all of the failings of ordinary souls, and I find, therefore, that all of the misconceptions that I was cherishing have been replaced by proper understanding. Now, by the grace of Your causeless mercy, I can remember who I really am and understand my obligations in service to You. I am fully prepared to do whatever You expect of me. Just say the word and I shall act!' " (73)

Sanjaya then concluded his narration:

"I am thrilled to the very core of my heart and filled with wonder and excitement after hearing this divine conversation between the supreme soul, the son of Vasudeva, Shri Krishna, and His exalted pure devotee, Arjuna, the valiant son of the noble Queen Kunti. (74)

It is only by the divine grace of my spiritual master, Vyasa, who is himself a great saint and pure devotee of the Lord, that I have been enabled to overhear these sacred words of Lord Krishna spoken in private to His dear friend Arjuna. The Lord is indeed the supreme mystic, and all who are on the path of spiritual realisation are actually on the way to meet Him. (75)

Again and again the words of this sacred conversation arise in my memory, and I become overwhelmed with wonder and ecstatic bliss. (76)

Your royal Majesty, time after time I recollect the beautiful and enchanting form of our Lord, the redeemer of the world, and my heart is filled with delight upon gaining that glorious vision. (77)

It is my deep conviction that if Lord Krishna, Who possesses inconceivable potencies and is the Master of all Masters, and His friend Arjuna, who is the most skilful of archers, are both present in one place, then all wealth and opulence will be there in abundance. Supreme victory will surely be theirs, all glory will be theirs, and perfect righteousness will always dwell with them!" (78)

Printed in Great Britain
by Amazon